FOUR
WOMEN
a family memoir
ONE
CENTURY

FOUR
WOMEN,
a family memoir
ONE
CENTURY

LISA BRANDOM

MOON▲LAKE
PUBLISHING COMPANY
SILOAM SPRINGS, ARKANSAS

MOON▲LAKE
PUBLISHING COMPANY

14213 Lake Forrest Heights
Siloam Springs, AR 72761

Printed in the United States of America

Design by Joel Armstrong, Photography by Lisa Brandom

Library of Congress Cataloging-in-Publication Data
Brandom, Lisa
    Four Women, One Century: a Family Memoir / Lisa Brandom
       p. cm.
    ISBN 0-9755950-0-8

1. Brandom, Lisa—Family
2. Authors, American—20th century—Biography
3. Mississippi—Biography

PS3552.R36F6 2005
818.5409 B7341   2005107689

10 9 8 7 6 5 4 3 2
First Edition

Dedicated to
Nelson
who made the impossible dream
possible

(1921–2003)

Chapter One

"Hush Little Baby"

—Ethel Beatrice Roberts (1909)

Of necessity, one must remember the past—and the shadows within it.

Ethel closed her eyes in disgust. "Not again," she thought as she bit into the insides of her mouth to keep from screaming as he pulled her cotton drawers down with both hands and leaned her over the sink.

Her mind could only escape by continuing to sing the lullaby in her mind, over and over again, "Hush, little baby, don't say a word . . . ." After she sang the whole song in her head, she let her mind drift into other things until he finished with her.

"Hey, you out by a mile," Bud had called to Ethel just an hour earlier as she rounded second base on her way to third.

"You didn't tag me. You gotta tag me to make me out," Ethel insisted.

"You out, girl, and that's that."

Ethel trudged back to the home plate area and flung her-

self down on the grass. Bud, her brother, who thought it was his right to boss all the younger kids around since he was the oldest boy of the kids, strutted back to the pitcher's mound. "He always has the loudest voice," Ethel moaned under her breath. She wished for Maudie, who was actually the oldest in the Roberts family (and now McCrory family), nineteen now, but far too busy with her new husband, Luther, to be much interested in playing baseball any more. If she could only have that familiar voice that used to side with her. Ethel was fifteen now and perhaps should have been more like Maudie. Maybe she ought to be seeing about getting herself a boyfriend too. She was such a tomboy, though, that the thought of her miraculously turning into a princess seemed a little silly to her. It was ludicrous to her to imagine herself as Cinderella and meeting Prince Charming. She didn't know if she could ever love a man.

It was late summer of 1909 at the family homestead in Carroll County, Mississippi. The month of August was always humid and suffocating even in the hills, but toward the end of day, the heat would let up a little bit, making it at least bearable for playing a game of ball. The katydids were singing their usual rhythmic blues number, the music of the hills, as all Southerners know. The humidity was its usual ninety percent with the temperature matching it even at seven o'clock in the evening. Ethel wiped the sweat from her face with the coattail of her cotton flowered dress Mammy had made for her. "Not a breath of air anywhere," she thought.

It was tradition for everyone in this neck of the woods to gather at the Roberts' house for late-afternoon ball games followed by watermelon, just gathered from the patch beside the house and put into wooden barrels with blocks of ice to chill. The watermelon meat had always made Ethel sick, but she still liked to chew it, swallow the cold juice, and then spit out the pulp. It wasn't much different from her brothers, Bud and Dell, who just thrust their faces into the middle of a hunk and then spit the seeds all over the ground.

Some of the other kids had to walk a mile or two to get there, but there was usually a crowd of smelly boys every night, and every now and then another girl would show up. Their mamas knew how hard everybody worked in the fields (including the girls) and let up on them when night came, insisting to their men on letting the kids play. "You let them boys go play. Them's only going to be kids once," they said in unison as the kids waited on the stoop for word to let them run over to the Roberts' in their dirty overalls with no shirts across the fields, hardly feeling the rocks under their bare feet.

While Ethel was sitting on the grass, worrying a little about the chiggers that might be biting her and thinking she'd do better with her next batting chance, she started thinking about her real daddy, not Tull, who would never, ever be her real daddy. Since Bud was the first-born boy, he was not only the boss of the kids but also the namesake of the family—George Pearson—but he had always been called by his nickname. Ethel's daddy,

George Franklin Roberts, had been a big voice in the little com-
munity of Pisgah and owned a lot of land while he was still
alive. Farming was so good he was even able to afford to hire a
foreman, Tull McCrory, to oversee most of the farm, so that he
could take it a bit easier as he got older. He didn't even begin
his family with Ida Jane Slocum until he was thirty-three years
old. She was just a kid, though, when they married and was not
even eighteen when Maudie was born. George Franklin had
been forty-three when his last child, Dell, was born. There had
been five kids in ten years. It seemed when Ida Jane quit nurs-
ing one, another one came along.

Both he and Ida Jane were of Scotch-Irish descent and
were leaders of the little community church. He had even donat-
ed some of his land to the church for its building and cemetery.
Ida Jane routinely took the babies to church practically from the
moment they were born. In fact, all the women would place their
babies, ranging in age from the smallest to toddlers, on blankets
at the rear of the building. Whenever one would cry, the mama
would go back and tend to him or her.

After her daddy died, Tull, "the man of the cigars and pot
belly," thought Ethel, simply saw a chance to bed a lonely
woman and perhaps get himself a farm, all to himself, for the
rest of his life. Ethel's life had been trying since he became her
stepfather a few years back. Other than her mama, she was the
only girl around. Maudie and Luther still lived close but not
close enough that Ethel could routinely run over and tell her

problems to her. There was certainly no way she could tell Mammy, and the boys wouldn't believe her anyway.

While she waited for her turn to bat the ball again and hopefully make a home run to show Bud what a good player she really was, Ethel began to think of Clidie Mabel, her sister. She could have talked to her if she was still alive. She would have been thirteen now, and they had been so close when they were little kids. She almost became mad when she thought about Clidie leaving her here. As she looked up at the clouds, she tried to imagine Clidie as a thirteen-year-old. "Why, she's up there in heaven just floating around all day without a doggone thing to do," Ethel imagined. She herself was so tired that her body ached just thinking about all the household chores she still had to do when she went in. She wondered what Clidie felt, being dead and all. The thoughts kept etching themselves in her memory as if an unseen hand kept writing and writing and wouldn't let her forget that day six years ago.

It was the second week of December in 1903 when Clidie got burned. The big monthly washing was taking place outside her house in the black kettle. The clothes were stacked, as always, on a makeshift table in the front yard. The scent of homemade lye soap was strong enough to make your nose tickle. The clothesline already was weighted down by a few freshly laundered clothes, blankets, and sheets. The boys' job was to build the fire while the girls and Mammy scrubbed the dirty clothes on the old washboards to get the stains out.

The weather was a bit chilly for Mississippi, and the day was gray and cloudy. Christmas was just two weeks away. They were all looking forward to going to church on Christmas Eve and exchanging their presents. Everyone knew you couldn't do that, however, with dirty clothes on. How could you possibly thank God for baby Jesus if you had dirty clothes on? "You have to be as clean on your body as you are in your heart," Mammy had told Maudie, Ethel and Clidie. Mammy had decided to get everything all washed up before winter in Mississippi truly set in.

"This is the way we wash our clothes, wash our clothes, wash our clothes," the three girls sang in unison. It was either that child's song or another of their favorites, like "I'm forever blowing bubbles, pretty bubbles in the sky." They couldn't resist taking a handful of bubbles and coating each other's clothes with them.

On one of the trips out to the black, boiling kettle, with an armful of dirty clothes, Clidie had gotten too close to the boiling cauldron.

"Mammy, Clidie's on fire!" Ethel tried to scream but found her voice had shrunk into a childlike panicky one that she didn't recognize.

Mammy heard Ethel though, as mamas are trained to do when their daughters are in danger. She immediately rolled her little daughter on the ground over and over again until the fire was out. She hollered then to eleven-year-old Bud, "Bud, get your daddy out of the field. Clidie's been burnt. Then run get the doctor as fast as your legs will carry you." Ethel until the day she died would never forget the agonizing screams from Clidie for two days and nights before she died; they were cauterized into her brain, she knew. To this day, Mammy still kept Clidie's burned and tattered dress in her hope chest and would take it out every now and then and just sit and stare—sit and stare—at it.

Shortly after Clidie left them, Ethel was near death herself from a bad case of typhoid fever. "I must have drank some of the bad water that the old geezers here in the county warned us about," she thought. She had to stay in bed for six weeks and even had to learn how to take steps again like a little bitty baby. When she was most delirious, she would cry out to Mammy by her bed, "Just let me go, Mammy. It won't be too bad."

Ethel's reverie about her Daddy, sister, and herself was interrupted on the ball field right as it came time for her finally to bat. Her Mammy's voice sounded urgent. "Ethel, come inside and rock the baby."

After her Daddy died and her mama married Tull, it wasn't long before another baby girl had come along to help soothe mama's mind and heart. Murry was born just a mere three and one-half years after Clidie died and Elise just a couple of weeks ago. Mammy still wasn't back up to par, though, and stayed in the bed a lot. Elise's cradle was beside her and Tull's bed, so she could reach over and rock it. Sometimes, though, Elise would have colic. She'd stretch her little body tight and scream. Then Mammy would call, "Ethel Beatrice, come inside and rock the baby."

"Why wasn't I born a boy?" Ethel thought as she reluctantly trudged up the steps of the farm house, with her head down, as was her lifelong habit, picked up baby Elise from her cradle where she was still screaming, and walked over to the corner of the big room to the rocking chair. "They think they're so smart and can do and say anything they want and can get away with it all."

Elise hushed up instantly as Ethel cradled her in her arms. She couldn't be mad at this precious baby girl, though, who seemed to be looking up at her now all happy after having been rescued from her plight in the cradle. She even seemed to have one of those tiny smiles on her face, which newborns get. "Her little lips are so sweet. Maybe one day, I'll actually have one of these myself," she thought.

"Hush, little baby, don't say a word. Mama's gonna to buy you a…."

She paused as she heard the door to the side of the house creak open. She prayed to God that it wasn't Tull again, "Please, God, please don't let it be him." She smelled his body odor, though, a mixture of sweat and cigars and knew otherwise.

"I'm just coming in for a drink of water. We've got another hour or so before I can let those damned, lazy niggers in the field quit for the day. Your brothers get to play their infernal ball game every night, though. Yor Mama thinks that's good for 'em," Tull was grumbling.

"Put that baby down, girl, and come over and give your

Daddy a drink, and a hug too while you're at it."

"STEPFATHER," Ethel screamed in her mind.

Elise had just gone to sleep and allowed her half-sister to place her back into the cradle without a murmur. She could hear Mammy gently snoring upstairs in her bed. Ethel went to the sink where there was a bucket of well water still cool that she had drawn from its watery blackness just a short while before supper.

Tull came up behind her and put his hot hand underneath her long, flowered house dress. "Girl, you better be good to me, and you'd damn sure better be quiet, or I'll run you out of this house quicker than a coon can climb a tree. You're not too good for it."

One thing she knew: Tull was certainly not her idea of Prince Charming.

Chapter Two
"Don't Say a Word"
—Ethel Beatrice Roberts Hatley (1918)

Walter wasn't exactly Ethel's idea of Prince Charming either when she married him at barely twenty years of age; he was simply convenient. All the Hatleys were peculiar, she thought—Walter's parents, Walter, his twin brother, and all the other relatives. "But," she rationalized to herself, "they are at least familiar peculiar." What she meant by that was that they had grown up together in Carroll County, Mississippi; she knew all his idiosyncrasies well; she chose to marry him anyway. He didn't talk much, and when he did, it was primarily about the weather or the crops.

He was more of a reason to leave home, though, than Daddy Tull was an incentive to stay any longer. The two of them had gotten married on March 15, 1914. They had gone in to the Justice of the Peace, C. M. Garrard, for a small, private ceremony. She and Walter had started school together in 1902. Both their fathers were farmers like practically everybody else in the county. Both had met all of society's expectations up to this time in their lives. They went to school for the usual eight years and then had a big graduation ceremony from eighth grade to cele- brate the completion of their formal schooling. Everybody was older at that time at the end of eighth grade because of the loss of time from school to help out on the farms during the school years. Walter continued to help out at his daddy's farm like always, hoping eventually to buy some of the land for a place of their own and to make sure Ethel started having the requisite babies.

As she thought about it, Ethel realized she couldn't explain to anybody exactly why she HAD married him, other than that it just seemed to be the thing to do shortly after they graduated. What else could a woman do? Maudie was married to Luther, Bud was married to Ellie, and she was the next one down the line. They both worked not only from sunup to sundown, never needing a clock, but also sometimes even by the light of the oil lamps—she in the house cooking, cleaning, sewing, washing all day long, even into the night while he worked in the fields.

They started a family almost immediately—Lord knows she had plenty of experience taking care of the two little ones, Elise and little Murry, the last few years, but they were now nine and eleven. She wondered if all men were like Daddy Tull. She hoped not and prayed she and Walter could make a life together.

And they had at least begun one before the will of God took them in another direction. It was the winter of 1918 when it happened. Ethel smiled to herself as she looked at her two beautiful little chaps. James Robert, her firstborn, had come along in 1916, and Walter Frances, her baby daughter, was just a few months old. Both had her coloring—coal black hair and brown eyes—and, thankfully there was no sign of that Hatley peculiarity in them other than in Frances, who was already a bit of a problem baby—all colicky and fussy, wanting to be rocked and nursed all the time.

Ethel sat in the corner of their little house, holding Frances with one arm as she nursed her and cradling her Bible in her other arm. It was near impossible to get a few minutes each day to study it. "Hush, little baby, don't say a word..." Ethel hummed the familiar lullaby to Frances that was second nature to her—just as she had sung it to Elise and Murry. Walter would be coming in for his supper soon.

Frances arched her back and screamed even louder. Ethel placed her hand on the child's head and felt her; she seemed a little too hot. A fear went through her mind, but just momentarily. It was as if these children were the only ones who could give her solace in this broken-up world; they were her creations, the marrow of her life. She was obsessed by them at times, she thought. She thought of the Scripture in Ecclesiastes that talks about a threefold cord, which couldn't be easily broken. Her preacher said that verse was supposed to represent the woman, her husband, and the Holy Spirit, but because of how much she loved her two little chaps, it could even refer to the three of them—her and the two babies.

She then started to humor herself a bit and get her mind away from these obsessive thoughts as she rocked and crooned to Frances. She started to think about her daughter's full name. Her teachers were going to be so confused when Frances got to first grade, and they wouldn't know whether to expect a girl or a boy. People often asked her, "Why'd you pick such a crazy name for a girl, Ethel?"

"I just wanted to honor my husband and give the baby his name," she'd reply coyly, as if there must be some additional mystery as yet unexplained. After all, she had been a Roberts before she married, and her son already had Robert as his middle name. It was only after the fact that she realized Frances had inherited a bit of the Hatley temperament.

The door to the house creaked slightly, and she involuntarily jumped, remembering an old dread from the past when she lived at home with Mammy and Daddy Tull. She shuddered and was mad at herself, for she had done her dead level best to block out those memories.

"Darn, it's cold outside—for a November Mississippi winter's day, that is—," Walter complained as he came inside the small frame house that belonged to his parents, shaking the snow from his rubber boots. His face was blustery red and chapped from the cold air. He'd been out checking on the condition of the fences around the place. In winter, the farm incessantly needed repairs of all sorts. He and Ethel and the babies had been living in a little house on the Hatley place since they were married.

This type of house has always been known in the South as a shotgun house, the joke being that if somebody were to shoot a bullet through the front door it would come out the back—it was essentially two rooms and good enough for a couple starting out. It could be added on to as more and more children came along. The four of them were a little snug but cozy enough as long as Frances was still in her crib. James Robert slept by their bed on one side and Frances on the other. The ever-present Southern outhouse was in the back, and Ethel and Walter used slop jars during the night if necessary—especially during the cold weather.

"Go ahead and help yourself to some fixin's. Soup's in the pot, and cornbread's ready too. I think she's about to drop off now. She's given me a heap of trouble today with her bawling, and James Robert's been fussing too."

While the words from her lips sounded tough, Walter knew Ethel well enough after all these years growing up together to know not to take her complaints too seriously. Those babies were what she lived for. She was strong and good natured; crying babies were an inevitable part of being a mama.

"Hon, I really don't feel like eatin' anything tonight. I'm a little achey; I'm going to try and get warm. I'm chillin'." He stood with his backside to the hissing fire in the woodstove for a few minutes.

He then pulled some of the handmade quilts off the rack in the front room and put them around him as his teeth began to chatter loud enough even for Ethel to hear.

"Maybe if you could eat just a little soup, it'd warm you up after a spell," Ethel suggested.

"My throat is so raw and scratchy I couldn't swallow a bite if I tried."

They looked at each other and tried to put out of their minds the unspoken fear that had begun to haunt everyone in 1918. Its presence with them was as insidious and silent as a stranger intruding upon them in the dead of night. The neighborhood children had even begun to sing a jingle about a bird named Enza. She knew the lyrics and had heard Elise and Murry singing them, "I had a little bird, / Its name was Enza. / I opened the window, / and in-flu-enza." She shouldn't be so morbid, she again told herself, as she fought to cover up her own momentary chill.

"Let's get you under the covers in bed then, and I'll run out and fetch the doc for you."

"You can't do that, babe; it's night out, and the chaps here need you. I'll be all right tomorrow; I just need a good night's rest, I'm sure."

"Well, you can at least try some of my tea and molasses medicine. I'll fix it for you."

"Sure, whatever you say," Walter said feebly.

He seemed to settle on down in the feather bed and went

to sleep for several hours. After she got the children down for the night, she climbed in beside him and noticed that the chills had started again. "I can warm him up," she thought and even managed a smile as she thought of old King David in the Bible. He was so cold he couldn't get warm until the servants brought in a young woman to care for him and lie with him.

Walter, though, began to shake so violently that she thought he might actually fall out of their big feather bed. Finally, his body was still, but she noticed that his temperature seemed to be going way up. She thought he might rest better if he had the bed to himself, so she slipped out and crawled into James Robert's single bed. James Robert just mumbled a bit in his sleepy child dreams but didn't wake up. He felt so warm and babyish—just barely beginning to form sentences and express his personality. He was easy-going like she was generally (I'll have to allow him a fussy day or so every once in a while, she thought)—a child of her heart. His hair smelled like the lemons she had used in the shampoo water that day.

Her body was aching too, but not with illness—just exhaustion from the busyness of the day and night. She drifted off into sleep in mid-sentence as she was praying for Walter, "Lord, please, Lord. Please heal Walter and make him ... well ...."

In a few short minutes, it seemed to her, she awoke to see thin ice crystals forming on the bedroom window, dancing as if to welcome the end of the dark night. She saw shades of daylight impatiently bolting through the darkness of the room. "My gosh," she thought, as she popped up quickly, "Walter's usually up by now. I'd better get him up," Then she remembered—he had been sick the night before.

She patted James Robert's behind; he was breathing with that soft baby purring sound, with just a hint of huskiness in his chest. She peeped into the crib at Frances, who had finally started sleeping through the night and who, thankfully, wasn't stirring either.

"Walter, honey, wake up. You overslept."

There was a silence with no crumpling of the covers back. No stretching or wiggling of his toes. Nothing within stirred. She began to hold down a rising sense of panic within her.

"Honey, how are you feeling this morning?" Her voice was rising to a high pitch.

Ethel pulled back the covers and began to feel lightheaded as she stared at her husband. His body was as chilled to the touch as ice water left outside in a well bucket on a winter's day. He wasn't breathing. On the pillow beside him was a spot of bloody froth that had come from his lips. Ethel had seen death before—when her sister, Clidie Mabell, was lying in her wooden box in the parlor of the house before she was buried. She remembered her daddy too. She knew she had lost Walter.

Again, as when Clidie was burning, she could not manage to get her vocal chords to respond to her inward commands for help. She uttered a startled whimper only as she threw on her coat and galoshes and went running to her in-laws' house, leaving James Robert and Frances alone in their beds, failing even to close the door.

The next couple of days were practically obliterated from her memory. She was told by Elise that she had later gone to Mammy and Daddy Tull's house in a daze, blindly seeking help as if she hadn't already told the Hatleys. She was almost incoherent and kept mumbling, "Enza...our house. Enza's...house." Her mama, as she had always done in an emergency, quickly took charge of Ethel and the two chaps.

The two chaps, however, within a few short days, became one. James Robert also contracted the flu and died just as quickly as his father had.

The funerals, along with many others in Carroll County that year, were held quietly. A black wreath was simply hung on the front door, indicating that another one or more in the family had fallen victim to the Spanish flu pandemic of 1918. Ethel later read about the symptoms in the county newspaper and found they were always the same—general weakness, severe aches in muscles, backs, joints, and heads. Fevers like Walter's and James Robert's often soared immediately to 105 degrees. Physicians felt helpless trying to deal with patients whose lungs filled with blood and who died of pneumonia because their lungs could no longer provide air. People were healthy one minute and deathly sick the next. Carroll County, Mississippi, was not the only county to experience loss. Between 500,000 and 675,000 would die in America alone, with 20 to 40 million worldwide losing their lives that year.

After the funerals, Ethel went back to the shotgun house and sat in the rocker with Frances again. The surviving daughter, the little princess, the apple of her Mama's eye, for once in her life seemed to understand that this was the time for silence. She simply smiled up at her mama. "Fat little Frances," Ethel thought resignedly as she uncovered the baby's chunky little thighs. "Whatever are we gonna do now?"

She began to assess her options, none of which seemed satisfactory. She could go back home with Frances and live with her Mama, but the trouble was, that meant living in the same house with Daddy Tull again. She couldn't bear to think about his "man's needs," as he called them. No, that wasn't an option. She could pick up and go to Greenwood, just a few miles from home, maybe live in a boardinghouse, get a job (although doing what, she couldn't possibly imagine since women at that time were either school marms [she was hardly qualified with her eighth-grade education] or prostitutes). She could leave Frances with the Hatleys and take the train home every weekend to see her. She could get married again (after all that was society's expectation). She'd ask God to show her the way. She didn't have to decide anything just immediately.

"Hush, little baby, don't say a word. Mama's going to buy you a mockingbird. . . ."

Edna St. Vincent Millay would later write in her "Lament" poem the sentiments that Ethel was experiencing, "Life has to go on, / I forget just why."

Chapter Three
"Mama's Gonna Buy You…"
—Ethel Beatrice Roberts Hatley Rogers (1919)

And life did go on for Ethel for another sixty years, even though she really didn't believe it could then. "I can't do it. I can't do it," Ethel whispered under her breath as she sat, with her toddler Frances and Mammy close to the gravesides in the Pisgah Cemetery. The cemetery was located next to the little community church they attended.

"What would Daddy want for me?" she wondered.

It was May of 1919, a few months after the death of Walter and James Robert that cold, Mississippi winter before. She knew that her sorrow was not exclusive in Carroll County since countless others had also lost loved ones as she had, either through the war (the Great War, as it was ironically called—the War to End All Wars) or the Spanish influenza. Yet sorrow has a way of seeming exclusive—as if no other heart could experience being rent apart so fully. She had continued to live in the little shotgun house on the farm with Frances, but it was now time to begin thinking about a future for the two of them.

She smelled the scent of the blossoming flowers with the honeysuckle predominating. Some of the hyacinths and hydrangeas she knew had been planted along with the lilacs, but the honeysuckle grew wild, willy-nilly, over the tombstones. Nature was either planned or random, she thought, much like the botanical specimens before her. She had always had faith in God's goodness and mercy, but now she felt more wilted by life's surprises than anything else, and she wasn't sure what she believed. She had a lot of questions for God, and at this point, He seemed silent. She wanted to believe in Romans 8:28 and following—that everything worked to the good to those that love the Lord and are called to His purpose—but she wasn't sure she still believed it. She felt in her heart that she had indeed been separated from the love of God.

"I can't do it. I can't do it," she found herself chanting repeatedly as if to convince herself most of all that this thing before her was impossible, this "beast of the jungle" as Henry James called it. Mammy couldn't hear that well any more and was busying herself with the picnic dinner they had brought out to the cemetery. They both knew it was a last supper of sorts.

Frances just looked up at her Mama quizzically as if she were surprised to hear her voice—Frances with the straight black hair and brown eyes, who herself was changing at age ten months from a little baby look to a little girl look. Her mama didn't talk that much to her, so her voice almost startled her with its rhythmic sound and was somehow comforting. Ethel had gone about with her shoulders hunched the past few months, doing only the chores immediately required of her.

Even Mammy couldn't believe Ethel's words she had heard just the day before. Daddy Tull and the other kids weren't in the kitchen with them. It was the two of them only.

"Mammy, I've decided to go to Greenwood and get a job. I thought I'd leave Frances with the Hatleys and come home on the train to see her on the weekends," Ethel tentatively stated in order to get Mama's opinion and perhaps convince herself that she really would go.

"Do you have any idea what you're saying, Ethel? Don't you know how dangerous it is in town for a young gal like you? I know you've been through a lot the last few months, but is this the only way?"

"It's final, Mammy. I've made up my mind to go," Ethel responded nervously.

And go she did—all of eleven miles away to Greenwood, where she got a job immediately working for the telephone company. She was an operator and had to sit for hours before a strange-looking contraption with wires dangling all over, connecting calls and trying to remember everything all at once. She had little time even to think about what Frances might be learning from her peculiar in-laws, the Hatleys, and what additional bad habits she might be picking up from them. But Ethel did as she had promised her Mammy. Every weekend she dutifully took one of the two daily trains back to Carroll County.

She worked the night shift, so it was usually fairly quiet during the supper hours from five to eight p.m.. To earn her pay she was also required to be available in the front office in case anyone came in from the street to pay a bill. Since most folks still had an innate distrust of banks, the majority of transactions were in cash.

One evening about supper time she was enjoying a bit of quiet from connecting the usual number of callers to their parties when she heard the bell on the front door of the office jingle. She had just unwrapped her sandwich. She had finally learned to be calmer with unexpected interruptions, and there were a lot of them in this busy office. Someone had just strolled into the building and stood at the counter whistling, "It's a long way to Tipperary." She looked up to see a very tall, rather stout fellow who had come in to pay the telephone bill his mother had gotten the month before. His mother usually took care of this chore for a break from work more than anything else, but tonight Wyatt had offered to do it. He was going downtown for a haircut anyway. The barber shop had just closed at five p.m., and he felt in his pocket, remembering the money his mother had given him accompanied by the bill.

Wyatt was, as she would later learn, six feet, two and a quarter inches tall to her petite frame of five feet, four inches. His hair was beginning to thin already in spite of the fact that he was a mere twenty-two-year-old compared to her twenty-five years of life.

They had a brief conversation that first evening, sharing a casual conversation, common when two young people meet at the beginning of a relationship.

"Where is Tipperary anyway?" she asked after she put the money in the cash drawer.

"Heck if I know," he laughed.

In the months to come, Wyatt made it a point to return again and again with his mother's money and pay the bill each month in person. He had been in the war for almost a year and a half, from August 5, 1917, to December 23, 1918, had obviously seen a lot, likely participated in hell, and finally returned to Greenwood alive. In spite of all that, he was as scared as a squirrel in the road not knowing whether to keep running across or go back to where it came from. He wanted to ask this young woman out. Finally, though, he was able to "screw his courage to the sticking place," as Shakespeare had Lady Macbeth say, and ask her, with a bravado in his voice that he really didn't feel.

"Say, kiddo, you wanna go to the drugstore after you get off and have an ice cream soda? I think we'd have a swell time."

"Sure, why not? You seem like a fine fellow to me," she laughed, relieved that the courting had become official. She had found herself more relaxed about talking to folks, it seemed, since she started her work as a telephone operator.

As they got to know each other better, Wyatt became a one-man admiration society for the courage Ethel had shown. "Not many women of the time would be so brave," he said to her one night as he walked her back to her boarding house. But, in actuality, one of the reasons he had started to care for her so much was that he saw she had the same spirit as his mother had.

Wyatt's Mama was a strong woman too, it seemed, as Wyatt shared with Ethel her story over several nights. Her name at that time was Mrs. Polly A. Foggert—although his last name was Rogers. She would eventually have five husbands, the last of whom would survive her; Baas was his name. After her first husband, Mr. Rogers, died, leaving her with three young boys to raise (Wyatt was the oldest), she opened a boardinghouse to provide for them. She was a terrific cook, and she was assisted in her work by a black woman who was affectionately known as Aunt Mary. Wyatt and his brothers were quick to fall into line since Aunt Mary might as well have been called Sergeant Mary. She joined in the discipline whenever it was needed and gave the boys a swat in the appropriate places as they bounded into adulthood.

The table was always full for the eleven to fifteen boarders who ate three meals a day with her, along with Wyatt and his two brothers, Mitchell and Bill. The beds were always full as well, so they never lacked for anything after his Daddy died. Mrs. Polly also owned a butcher shop and could butcher a cow in a matter of minutes, it seemed. She had already taught the three boys this skill as well. "My Mama knew how to raise good boys. After all, she raised me," he teased, "and even though she can't read or write, she's smart. No one can beat her out of a dime."

Wyatt and Ethel decided they didn't want to rush their courtship and went along nice and easy for about a year, feeling their way through the murkiness of the deep water into which they were entering with all of its potential dangers. "Was life ever clear?" Ethel wondered. She didn't know if she could ever share with Wyatt what Daddy Tull had done to her through the years after he married Mammy (she never did). She didn't know if she could risk having another husband die on her; "It might be better to stay a widow," she rationalized to herself. She had already proven that she could live without a man if she had to. Other women did.

Wyatt also had a lot of gear to rid himself of after the Great War. He had volunteered for the war effort after the United States got into it in April of 1917. At first he didn't think he would since he asked himself what the assassination of the Archduke Francis Ferdinand and his wife, Sophie, some three years before had to do with a farm boy in Mississippi. He had also been disappointed in President Wilson, who ran for his re-election with the campaign slogan, "He kept us out of war," and yet asked Congress to declare war on Germany shortly after he won the vote again. Yet Wyatt, along with countless other boys his age, enlisted because this was America, and it was the patriotic choice to make. Before he left, he and his Mama stood outside their place in Greenwood for a photograph; she stood in her white dress with her arm inside his while he stood—an erect soldier at attention in his uniform, Army hat, and boots. Neither was smiling, and both were aware of the potential dangers and outcomes for them both should he fail to return.

When he returned to the States just two days before Christmas in 1918, he was as lost as Krebs in Hemingway's story, "Soldier's Home," when at first he "did not want to talk about the war at all. Later he felt the need to talk but no one wanted to hear about it." Mama and the two younger boys had never been out of the state of Mississippi. How could they possibly understand the horrors of trench warfare that seemed interminable or the Battle of Verdun, which went on for an ordeal of ten months with neither side gaining an advantage? How could they know what it was like to see and fear the sensation of mustard gas being used by both sides to kill one another, rendering even the gas masks useless? Sometimes it would hang for days over the trenches, and sometimes it would blow as easily back over them instead of the enemy and kill their boys. It was random. Assuming he could conquer these demonic giants of the Great War, could he marry a woman three years older than himself who already had a child by another man and who had giants of her own to deal with?

These were the questions that haunted them both as they explored the answers. Little by little, step by step, they eased into a relationship that would flower and grow just as surely, just as deeply, as the flowers in the cemetery that day Ethel had considered her future. They decided to knit their lives into a new three-fold cord, braiding and binding themselves together for life. On May 7,

1921, Mr. J. W. Rogers took for his beloved wife, Mrs. Ethel B. Hatley, in the presence of the minister of the Christian Church in Greenwood, W. O. Hornbaker.

And for the first time in her life, Ethel started to believe that fairy tales can come true and that God wasn't so far away from her after all.

Chapter Four
"A Mockingbird"
—Walter Frances Hatley Rogers (1923-1924)

God, in fact, was so close that Ethel saw Him each day, she thought, in the face of the little princess she and Wyatt were raising. Ethel called, "Frances, get out of bed. Today's the first day of school, remember. Frances, wake up. Are you sick?"

The early morning sun crept into the section house in Clarmont, Mississippi, on a hot August morning in 1923. Frances' Mama had just left the kitchen for a minute while she was preparing the usual big breakfast for her husband, Slick. Mama had taken lately to calling Daddy that instead of Wyatt like she used to. Shortly after they married, his hair had become so thin that in the last couple of years Mama had given up and joined in with the rest of his family and friends, calling him by his new nickname. She stood in Frances' bedroom, which was cluttered with clothes and toys everywhere.

It seems like Mama always thought Frances was sick if she didn't jump out of bed immediately. She had heard the story about her big brother and her real daddy, but it was hard for her to make a connection to people she had never even known.

Frances stirred slightly and turned back over in the bed—her black, short, straight hair sticking out of the sheet she had pulled over her around five a.m. when the sultry, sticky air began to let up slightly. "I'm not going," she announced.

"Of course you are. You've got to be a big girl. All big girls go to school. You know that."

"I don't," Frances lazily responded, "I hate mornings."

In spite of her numerous protests and her litany of complaints—she couldn't find the right colored stockings she needed for her blue jumper that Mama had made for her on this special day, she was convinced she had a stomachache, she hollered because her hair bow had gotten wrinkled the last time she wore it— an hour or so later Frances climbed into the seat of the Model T Ford that Mama and Daddy drove. She sulked all the way there and frequently kicked her feet at the dash in front of her, refusing to acknowledge Mama's role as family cheerleader about how much fun she was going to have and how much she was going to learn.

"Just think, Frances, you'll soon be reading much better than your Daddy and me. You know your real Daddy and I only finished the eighth grade."

It was only a mile to the one-room school building in Clarmont. She at least knew why her Mama was so excited. She had been practicing her driving so that she could get a driver's license and drive her to school every day. Not many families had a car in 1923, and even fewer women drove.

"I wish she hadn't learned," Frances thought to herself, "Maybe then I could've stayed home. I hate getting up in the morning. It's way too early."

Mama pulled up to the front door of the country schoolhouse. All the other kids seemed to know one another already and were standing with their lunch pails together in little groups talking. They seemed a little taken back by this woman in her Model T and began to stare at the two new arrivals.

"I don't know anybody here," Frances panicked and started demanding in her loudest voice, "Take me home, Mama!"

Her mama tried to comfort her; she knew she should just drive away after she got Frances out and settled, but then she had a glimpse of a memory from the past. It was that winter's morning in 1918 when she realized her personal sun, the light of her life, had been extinguished and that she had lost James Robert forever. She knew she wouldn't make Frances go to school now if she didn't want to.

She thought about Slick's reaction but knew he would support her decision since there weren't going to be any more babies. Shortly after she and Slick had gotten married in 1921, she was rushed to the hospital in Clarksdale for surgery. She woke up, saw tears in Slick's eyes, and knew all. "Why shouldn't I let Frances have another year at home with me? What does it really matter in the long run?" she rationalized in her mind.

"Okay," she whispered comfortingly into Frances' ear, "I'll take you home." She stepped on the gas, leaving clouds of dust behind.

And home Frances went, and stayed there, for the next year with her Mama and Daddy, and everything was good again. Elise and Murry would ride over practically every day to see her. They usually rode to high school on horseback and would often stop by to play with her on their way back from school. She knew she was spoiled, but she didn't care. She, Mama, and Daddy had such fun together. They all went to church every Sunday. The only part of her life she dreaded, other than eventually having to go to school, was having to see Daddy Tull when she went over to Mammy's. It seems as if he was always sitting in his big stuffed chair offering all the little girls in his life the opportunity to get two bits by sitting in his lap.

"Come here, Frances. Get up in my lap. I've got this pretty silver quarter for you if you do."

She was lured only once. As she climbed onto Daddy Tull's lap, it seemed as if his hips were in motion and his breathing heavier than usual. Everybody else was in the kitchen eating apple pie and drinking coffee. He wore his usual clothes— a white T-shirt and some khaki pants. He smelled of the endless train of cigars that he smoked and the snuff he dipped. His spittoon was always beside the chair. He slipped his hand underneath her dress and started pulling her drawers down.

"Stop that this minute, you old goat," Frances hollered, jabbing her elbow into his ribs with all her might and jumping down from his lap. "Don't you ever do that again!"

And he didn't—to her at least. In general, life for the Rogers family was good, and no changes in one's routine—like school—seemed to be necessary in Frances' mind.

Soon, however, the next August came along, 1924, and the scene from a year ago was repeated down to the smallest of details with the exception of one. Just as Frances was all tuned up to cry loudly again and refuse once more to go in, a strange little girl walked up to her Mama.

"Hi, my name is Mary Louise. I'm in fifth grade, and I'll take her inside."

"Oh, I'd be ever so grateful if you'd do that. This gal's a handful," Ethel replied.

The little girl gently took Frances' hand and spoke to her in the quietest of voices. "If you'll go in with me, I'll stay with you all day. You don't have to be afraid," she whispered.

Frances was so startled by this new and novel approach that she assented. Had she not gone in that day into the one-room school with its one teacher, Frances might not have ever gotten her education.

In the next couple of years, the school was expanded into two rooms, and another teacher was hired. Frances had settled into her school routine by then, and she and Mary Louise remained the best of friends in spite of their age difference.

Mary Louise became a lifelong friend from the very beginning.

The teacher who was hired for the new classroom turned out to be no one else other than her Aunt Elise. By this time, Elise had graduated from high school, wearing a lovely white chiffon dress for her graduation ceremony, and gone to college for a year. She was then qualified to teach in a small, country school with five grades. She lived with Frances, her half-sister and her husband for one whole school year until she married Dewey, whom she had met when she was in college. Life was good for Frances again—for a brief while until she and Elise started to cross ways.

Frances was a hefty little girl when she was in grade school. Both her parents loved to eat, and Mama cooked good meals with lots of meat like fried ham and fried chicken plus fried okra, fried corn, and fried potatoes. Her Mama and Daddy had both put on a little weight, but since they worked so hard— he on the railroad as a section foreman there in Clarmont and she at home doing all kinds of household chores—they were able to work off most of their extra calories.

Frances, however, by this time had become a lover of books. When she wasn't sitting for eight hours at school in her desk, she was lying in her bed at home reading some of the great classics Mama was buying for her like *The Adventures of Tom Sawyer*, O'Henry's short stories, which always had those surprise endings, and a little Nathaniel Hawthorne, although she felt he was a little too stuck on those Puritan ancestors of his.

For lunch every morning, Mama packed her goodies into the lunch pail—four sandwiches, a piece of cake, an apple, and a nickel to buy a Coke. Once Elise started teaching at the school, however, she began to insist that Frances get one sandwich, one apple, and one Coke. She laid down the McCrory law for her half-sister, and nothing would deter her from her goal—a slimmer niece. It became a battle of three wills, not a tightly knit braid this time.

"I can't live on that, Mama!" Frances fumed. "I'm gonna starve to death if that's all I get to eat every day."

Elise intervened, "And not only that, Ethel, but you need to stop driving this child to school every day. Let her walk; it's just one mile. She needs the exercise."

"What are ya'll trying to do—kill me?" Frances' voice got louder and louder until it was a high-pitched yell.

"Maybe I should give her…maybe…one more sandwich. It won't hurt her to have one more," Ethel responded as she looked at Elise as if she needed to ask permission about how to raise her own daughter.

"No, she gets one sandwich and one only. Do you want her to be fat forever? Look at her; she's a slob," Elise's voice itself rose higher and higher until it was several decibels over Frances' wailing. The Jews at the Wailing Wall couldn't have competed with the both of them.

For once in her life, Frances lost the battle but won the ultimate victory. She continued in the next few years to be the dominant general of the three in her immediate household, and her happiest memory of this time was Elise moving out of their house and her school to marry Dewey. Frances was most comfortable being the little princess again.

The 1920s were her happiest days, Frances often thought. She was just a happy kid. She, Mama, and Daddy would drive out to a big lake and go swimming every weekend in the summer, go back home for hamburgers, and then go to a movie. "This's my idea of heaven," Frances would say to herself. She could learn about the world outside Clarmont (and Clarksdale, six miles north) in the movies. She really knew nothing about the gangsters in the cities like Chicago, nothing about prohibition in the United States (her family were good country people and non-drinkers), nothing about the businessmen in New York who were jumping out windows when the depression hit in 1929. She went to lots of old movies with her Mama and Daddy, silent ones and the first talkies. She saw the first one that ever came out, *The Jazz Singer* with Al Jolson, and later was as amazed, and disappointed, as the rest of the country when Rudolph Valentino's high-pitched voice didn't fit his macho image of an Arabian sheik. She learned of the world outside of her own personal reality in the movies. Life was good. Mama had not only promised her a mockingbird; she had given it to her.

Chapter Five
"If That Mockingbird Don't Sing. . ."
— Walter Frances Hatley Rogers (1932-1936)

And that mockingbird seemed to be forever singing. "We can't, Daddy, we just can't move again! I'm not going; I'm simply not going to do it," was Frances' initial reaction to her stepfather's words.

"I'm sorry, honey, but a man's got to do what a man's got to do," Frances' Daddy was saying to her as she stared up at him in disbelief.

Frances didn't know much about the reality of the Depression in the years 1932, 1933, 1934, and 1935; she just knew that it was making her life miserable. She sometimes got a glance at Daddy's newspapers or heard the news on the radio about how difficult the times were for everybody in America. She had plenty to eat though; in spite of Elise's plan to slender her up a bit, she was still a bit on the chubby side. So stories of unemployment the old men at the store sat around and talked about were just plain boring. What did bother her, though, was the fact that

Daddy had to move her and Mama all the time now, from place to place in order to keep his job. Every time that happened she had to make friends all over again.

Daddy's job at Illinois Central Railroad as a foreman meant that he had earned some seniority since he had worked for them since 1922. Because of the Depression, those who had more seniority than he did could "roll" him. Daddy explained, "That means, Frances, that anybody with more seniority than I got gets to take my job if they want it, and I have to find somebody to roll so that I can keep a job."

"That means then, Daddy, that we're going to have to move from Clarmont, and I'm going to have to leave all my friends," Frances wailed as the reality of the Depression finally began to make an impression.

Frances had just completed part of her eighth-grade year when she, Mama, and Daddy had to pack up and move to Savage. She was going to miss not only her friends, her swims, and her movies, but also her horseback rides. One of the rich landowners in Clarmont owned a stable of horses and always let the country kids ride them whenever they wanted. She had been riding since she was eleven with a neighbor boy who had taught her and would saddle her horse for her. "Gosh, we have fun—riding several hours or half a day together with the wind blowing through our hair and feeling free as birds," Frances was thinking as she heard Daddy mouth the words about the move. "How can I give up all that?"

But Frances got a surprise, after the move. Instead of being miserable, she found herself having the time of her life at her new home in Savage. It hadn't taken long at all for her to meet new friends, and it was so much fun riding the school bus to Arkabutler eight miles up into the hills. The train came into town in the morning and at night. All the young folks (as well as the old people) met the train in order to socialize. If one had a boyfriend (as Frances always did), he'd be at the train. "See you at the train," she and her friends would all say to one another and wink. "We'll have a swell time."

After the train came in the morning, everyone walked over to the tiny post office and waited for the postmistress to put the mail up. It didn't matter if she and her friends didn't receive any mail because every day they saw the friends they wanted to see anyway. For graduation her eighth-grade year, Frances thought she was gorgeous in Elise's white chiffon dress as she twirled around and around in front of the mirror. She loved to look over her shoulder and smile that cute little smile she practiced at everyone.

This same year in 1932 Frances discovered boys, not just "friend" boys but boys who might even kiss her one day, or better yet, walk her down the aisle. One of these early boyfriends, whose name was Cooter, wrote her a letter (which she picked up at the post office; she was glad everyone was there to read it with her), asking if he could come to Savage (an eight-mile trip for him) along with his sister and take her to church one night.

"Mama, Daddy, can I go? Please, please, please say I can!"

"I don't know," Mama had said. "Aren't you a little too young to be so independent, missy?"

But in the end, both her Mama and her Daddy relented (as they always did when Frances' voice level got high enough). She remembered how painfully shy Cooter was as he came to pick her up in his Model A Ford. He couldn't even look at Mama and Daddy when he came to the door. He seemed to think his shoes were the most fascinating objects in the world.

"Is Frances ready to go?" he mumbled.

She knew Mama and Daddy must have been laughing and peeping out behind the lace curtains as the car disappeared on the dusty country road toward his church.

At church, he took a lot of kidding from everybody because she was his first girl. "Hey, Cooter, who's that you got with ya?"

"Bring her over here and let me meet her, will ya?"

"Cooter, why you so dressed up tonight? You even smell good for a change."

After the church service was over, he drove the full eight miles to his house, let his sister out, and the two of them drove back to Savage alone. "Frances, can I kiss you?" Cooter asked as he leaned over toward her, taking his eyes from the road for a brief second only.

"Cooter, watch the road!" Frances hollered out just in time to see the car careening into a ditch.

For that next year, Cooter became her official boyfriend. The kidding continued even from the high school basketball coach, who announced to everyone one day in chapel that Cooter was so anxious to get back to Frances he couldn't think straight about what he was doing.

"I almost died on the spot," she remembered. "I was mortified."

But it was still the Depression, and once again, Daddy got rolled and, therefore, had to roll a younger guy in order to keep food on the table for the three of them, and that included a significant amount for Frances. In 1933 the Rogers family moved on to Lake Cormorant. She and Cooter wrote for a while, but by this time Frances had finally understood the principle of rolling and decided to roll Cooter for another boyfriend.

The new place was small like Savage, but the best part of all was that it was a mere sixteen miles to Memphis. Instead of going to the train or to the post office for entertainment, they actually went to TOWN where there was always something going on. There were movies again and boxing matches (Daddy loved them; she now found herself calling him Pop more and more now—which seemed more sophisticated to her). Also, she was now dancing on the Claridge Roof with her new boyfriend, whose name was Bruce. He was the one who had taken her there for the first time.

Bruce lived next door to her in Lake Cormorant. He had been away at school when they first moved there and was two years older than she. Frances had fallen immediately in love with the guy. To him, though, she was more like a kid sister, always teasing and taking her places. "Hey, kid, you wanna go up to the Claridge this Saturday night and hear Henry Bussi and his orchestra play? Do a little dancing on the rooftop?"

Her heart felt like a wildly bouncing ball. "Sure I'd like that." She tried not to be either too enthusiastic nor too kid like in her response, but she loved Henry Bussi since she listened to him on the radio all the time. She was thrilled at the thought of dancing to his music with the man she worshipped. Bruce was her first true love. To him, however, she remained a kid, and he simply deflated that wildly bouncing ball of a heart for the first time in her life. She was willing to settle, though, for what he would choose to give her. When Mama announced in just a few short months that they were once again moving, this time to Lambert, she cried again.

"Frances, there'll be other boys. He's not the only crawdad in the pond."

"Never, never, never like Bruce though, Mama!" Frances wailed.

When the three of them got to Lambert, they had to live in an apartment since it was again another tiny town, and Pop didn't get a section house with this new job. It was around the corner from the Freeman family who had three kids—Lois, Nelson, and Doris. It was Lois (not Mary Louise this time) who was asked by their landlady to take Frances to school with her the next day. Lois was Frances' age, Nelson was a mere thirteen-year-old kid, so she never bothered about noticing him, and

Doris was just six. Their Mama, who was nicknamed Mimi by everyone, was a heck of a cook, so Frances hung around next door at their house a lot. Lois and she were best friends and graduated from high school together at Lambert High School in 1936.

The dances continued, not at Memphis, but in a mammoth space there in Lambert where a small orchestra from Memphis would come down and play nearly every weekend. There were the usual school plays and high school football. Her happiest time was in her senior year when she was named "Miss Lambert High School" and voted the cutest girl in the high school. "I am in seventh heaven!" Frances thought and was extremely glad just to be alive to enjoy the honors. The year before, though, her life had been in doubt.

In her eleventh-grade year, something awful had happened to her. She had been to a party the night before with her new boyfriend, whose nickname was Nub (an odd nickname admittedly, but several years back when he was hanging out at the national guard armory there had been a terrible explosion of some type which resulted in his losing three fingers on his right hand; therefore, the cruel nickname had resulted, although his mother continued to call him by his rightful name, Leonard). Frances thought this boyfriend was the love she had always wanted. He was twenty-two (five years older than she), had a year in college already, and a job.

She woke up that morning feeling sick and nauseated with awful pains in her stomach. "Frances, are you sick?" Mama called into the bedroom with her usual question. "Get out of bed. It's Saturday. You can't sleep all day long," Mama fussed.

"I can't, Mama, I really am sick. I feel so bad. I hurt all over."

"You just ate a lot of junk food last night at the party. That's the only thing wrong with you. I've told you over and over again not to eat so much. Here, take this castor oil, and you'll feel better in no time I know."

By noon the pain for Frances was so bad that Mama began to feel that panicky feeling once again, but she tried to ignore it by singing to herself: "If that mockingbird don't sing, Mama's going to buy you a diamond ring."

She called the doctor, who came over, examined Frances, and concluded that she had appendicitis. Her Mama was so dependent on Pop for everything, though, that she couldn't make a decision about what to do until he came home at four p.m. from the railroad. By the time he got in, the pain had stopped.

"Let's get you to sit up, and then we can take you to the hospital. It wouldn't hurt to have the doctor look at you again," Pop said gently. "We'll bundle you up and take you right in."

"I can't move. I'm too sore to move."

The doctor said later at the hospital in Marks four miles away that the pain had stopped when Frances' appendix ruptured. Infection from the rupture had spread throughout her body.

"Mr. and Mrs. Rogers, I have to be frank with you. I don't know if Frances is going to make it through this," the doctor spoke to them in the hallway of the small hospital. "We'll just have to play a waiting game and see what happens. I have a friend who's a doctor in Memphis; I'm going to call him every night and get his advice. She's developed a blood clot in her leg. Even if she lives, I don't know if she'll ever walk again. "

Her Mama crumpled like a Raggedy Ann doll into the arms of Slick. She was determined, though, that she would not lose her only daughter and Pop his only stepdaughter. She prayed for God to spare her. "Please, dear God, please let Frances get well. I don't know what I'd do if I lost this young'un. She's spoiled, I know, and I promise I'll do better if You'll just let her get better."

Although she stayed in the hospital for thirty days, not only did Frances recover but she also danced again six weeks later. For her senior dance a year later, she had two dates—Bruce, her love from Lake Cormorant, and Nub, her new love in Lambert. "I really know I've died and gone to heaven!" Frances thought as she strolled into the auditorium where the dance was being held—with a handsome beau on each side of her. She dreamed of the day she would walk down the aisle with her prince, take his hand into hers, and say, "I do."

Chapter Six
"Mama's Gonna Buy You a Diamond Ring"
—Walter Frances Hatley Rogers Sims (1937)

She did not have to wait long for a prince to stroll into her world. "I'll be rich," Frances thought happily, not about marrying a prince, but about the new change in her dull life. "Now I can help Mary Louise and Gerard with my room and board." It was on September 7, 1937, that she heard the grandest news: She had gotten a job as a soda jerk at the drugstore in Clarksdale and would be making $10 a week. The newly married Hauer family, along with baby Jerry, had taken Frances in a few weeks earlier because they knew how bored she was living in Mikoma, four miles from Webb (not the middle of everywhere, but nowhere, Frances thought). Once again Pop had rolled someone, and she and her Mama had to uproot their lives yet another time. Her darling Nub (or Nubbin, as she liked to call him) was broke as usual and couldn't come to see her very often. She had stood the isolation for just so long since, once again, she didn't know anyone in the new little country town and couldn't even begin to muster a desire or inclination to meet new people any more in yet another move in an endless string of them.

"Please, please, please, Mama, I've just got to get out of this little town. Let me go see Mary Louise and Gerard for a little while," she pleaded as her Mama took a pan of cornbread out of the oven.

Ethel wondered why all Frances' crises came when she was getting dinner ready for Slick's arrival home at noon.

After Frances' usual amount of pleading, followed by her voice rising to its usual dramatic high pitch, Mama relented and sent her off by bus the next day, promising that she and Pop would come over to Clarksdale every chance they got and check on her. She could always go home with them any time if the job wasn't working out.

The drugstore was located in the heart of downtown Clarksdale. Frances' friend Perry said he'd teach her to be the best soda jerk in the world. The Cokes had to be mixed by hand with the Coke syrup put in a glass first, then ice added, and carbonated water as the final ingredient. Stir and "voila"—one had a Coke! But there were also shakes and malts and sundaes to learn about, and hundreds of people, it seemed, were coming in all day long ordering sodas and visiting with their friends either before or after the movie that was attached to the drugstore. She hoped she could do it.

Miss Carrie and Miss Lou, the managers, had a talk together, and they agreed with Perry that Frances could have the

job. She loved her work after she got the hang of it and especially loved all the activity, even though she was dead tired at the end
of each day. On a lot of days, she worked from eight in the morning until eleven at night. One night she counted 242 tickets from
the fountain! Some nights all she felt like doing after work was
taking a bath, sitting out on the porch for an hour or so looking
up at that glorious harvest moon, and thinking about her Nubbin.

"He's lazy," she could hear in her mind what Pop had said
to her about Nub. "He doesn't have any ambition! There's other
boys out there. You can do better."

She didn't agree with Pop's assessment, but as on other rare
occasions in her life, she didn't make any argument otherwise.
She and Nub were supposed to get married in a mere few days,
on September 19, and she still wasn't sure the wedding would
actually take place. He didn't have a steady job, but she knew he
was trying hard. He worked three part-time jobs—in an icehouse
delivering big blocks of ice for the iceboxes that everybody had
in their houses, at the lumber company, and at the grocery store.

She thought about their times together when she was in
high school in Lambert; he'd always appear at her house about
eight a.m. in his little red pickup and take her to school even
though it was all of two blocks away. "Who cares about making
money?" Frances would often say to Pop when he was delivering one of his lectures about ambition. "My two great loves are
dancing and eating, and you know, Pop, what a dream dancer
Nub is!" And he *was* trying to do better so they could start with

a little money saved as a married couple. He had spoken for a small house in Lambert where they'd live and was trying to gather a few pieces of furniture together for it.

Frances looked down at the half-carat diamond ring Nub had given her before she moved to Mikoma. "Love is all we need," she thought. She went back in to Mary's apartment and wrote these words in her diary:

"Our 3rd anniversary! And I love him ten million times more than I did 3 yrs. ago tonite." She couldn't wait until September 19. He had chosen that date because it was also the day and month on which he was born. It would be easy to remember their anniversary. But as the gods would have it, Frances thought, the date was postponed because Nub felt he had to make just a little more money before they could start out as a married couple.

"Frances, be patient; it'll just be a little while longer. We can hang on until then. I'm as anxious as you are, baby," he tried to convince her.

In her diary that night, she wrote, "I've had the blues all day. . . Wish I could see my darling. Think I'll write him."

Life went on as tirelessly as an automated cotton gin for Frances, speedily separating the seeds from the pure white yarn-to-be. She and her friends saw a lot of movies since the theater was right there where she worked. One of her favorites was "Souls at Sea." She also loved listening to the radio and eating and drinking Cokes and acting goofy with her friends Sybil and

Mary Louise.

Ten days after her planned wedding day had come… and gone, Frances was in the drugstore as usual on the night of September 29. It was Wednesday, and business was practically nonexistent in the middle of the week. Miss Carrie and Miss Lou had started trusting her with the fountain on her own. The door opened, and Pandora's box walked in. Frances, like the first woman, according to Greek mythology, was immediately curious about this man before her. Mike Sims was six feet tall with blond, curly hair, and she thought he was the best-looking man she had ever seen.

"Hey there, good-looking lady, how's about a Coke float?"

She looked into those baby blue eyes and saw within him almost instantly a vulnerability beneath his good looks and smooth talk. Where others might have seen bravado, she saw childlike innocence, a sweet spirit, and later a generous heart.

He started giving her a rush from that night on, and he was there at the drugstore every night to walk her home. It was about a mile to Mary and Gerard's apartment, so they had a lot of time to get to know one another. In their long walks on moon-lit evenings, when the katydids were about the only sound one heard as they strolled together arm in arm, Frances learned about his life and his hurts.

"I've got to tell you something, lady, about my past. I don't want to ever be anything but honest with you." Frances almost stopped breathing since she was not sure she wanted to hear secrets from another time and place. She sensed there was another woman, and she already felt jealous of her. She thought, though, that he was the squarest man with her she had ever met. On that fall evening he shared with her how his parents, Aylmer Belton Sims and Virgil Vashti Cooper Sims, had owned a big plantation in Victoria, Arkansas. His Mama evidently had been the brains of the family and traveled all through the South buying and selling in the timber business. She had died when he was just a baby, a mere two years old. The family legend was that she suffered from epileptic seizures and on one of her business trips had checked into the hotel at Tutwiler, Mississippi. During the night, she had a seizure and died. When the authorities investigated her death, they found she had tucked huge sums of money underneath her mattress.

Mike talked easily to Frances that night about his life and spent several long hours with her on the front porch as they sipped lemonade. He told her about his Daddy going through the money so quickly after his Mama died and his later farming out his four sisters, Ora, Lela May, Mary Grace, Pauline, and him (just like cattle) to other family members to raise. It seems the aunt who had gotten Mike to raise was described by everyone as "the meanest woman in the world." His uncle, on the other hand, sneaked around reversing his wife's decisions with Mike and slipped him money to try to compensate for the boy's mistreatment. He had gotten confused, he told Frances, and started doing some activities he shouldn't have. He had started gambling, and he had gotten a girl pregnant while they were in high school. Kizzie Waddell was her name. They never lived together, he told Frances, and he never loved her, but he felt like he had to do right by her and give the baby a name. They had gotten married; she soon gave birth to twin boys—Robert Belton and William Addison—and they divorced just as quickly.

Frances sighed, and wasn't sure what she had gotten herself in for, but up until this point of her life, no one had ever been so honest with her about real issues of life. She had been protected so by Mama and Pop; she didn't realize what hard times people could have. He had just endeared himself to her all the more, it seemed.

Somehow Nub got word about what was going on and started coming to Clarksdale three times a week to see her and do his best to talk some sense into her. Both men, each five years older than she, were as sweet as could be to Frances. She'd go out with one the first night and the other the next night. Each one had good arguments for why he should be the man in her life.

"I love them both," she cried to Mary one late night after Mike had left, when baby Jerry and husband, Gerard, were asleep. "What am I gonna do, Mary?"

Mary, the one who had been a lifelong friend, was also the rational, logical one and tried to help her understand her feelings. "What are some good reasons for you to marry Nub?" she asked in her quiet voice.

"Oh, I don't know. I guess because he's good and I've loved him practically all my life—for five long years. We've grown up together."

"Well, that's a good start. Why do you think you should marry Mike then?"

"Because he's so handsome! And he's got such a good sense of humor. You know what he said to me just today, 'Lady, I wouldn't trade you off for a million acres of guinea pigs, and that's a lot of guinea pigs, lady!' I almost melted!"

Nub one night—Mike the next. It went on that way for several weeks until Wednesday, October 27, when Mike proposed to her. That night she recorded in her diary, "Thought about Mike all day. He came in tonite 'bout 7:30. Looked so adorable. He met me at eleven & we came home. He is so sweet. He asked me to marry him tonite. Sounds silly but he was the sweetest most sincere person I've ever heard. I am completely surprised & confused."

The next night, however, in her diary she recorded these words: "Nub came and we had it out. We are going to be married before or by Xmas, anyway *For sure.*"

A new wedding date for Frances and Nub was set for November 28. Mike was "grand," according to Frances' diary, when she told him the news about her wedding date with Nub, and he wasn't deterred from still coming into the drugstore all the time and being with her. She laughed loudly when he said, "I've got 30 days—Lord, let me do no wrong."

On Wednesday, November 3, Frances broke a date with Mike since Nub was coming into town. Evidently, Mike was hurt enough that Frances wrote in her diary that he "*quit* {her} cold." The next day, she wrote, "My long day & it has been plain hell all day. I haven't even seen or heard of Mike & it's driving me crazy. I want to see Mike so & yet I know I shouldn't feel that way. He's gone now forever. I am so tired & worn out I could die & so miserable."

The next day, she wrote, "Tonite Mike came in. I couldn't believe my eyes. He looked like a million dollars. Nub came tonite & I broke off the engagement. I'm just *not ready.* Mike called me late tonite." She put her half-carat ring into an envelope and sent it back to Nub at Lambert.

She knew she wanted to get married; she just didn't know still to whom. All her other friends were tying the knot. Annie Ruth and Victor had gotten married on September 12, and Lottie and Jack on November 13. Was she ever going to get married? My God, she was 19 already. She had such fun with Mike on Tuesday, the 16th. They dressed up like "Mr. & Mrs. Astorbilt" and went to the show to see *Prisoner of Zenda.*

On November 17, she surprised herself by impulsively doing the unthinkable. Mike was in the drugstore as usual being himself, and she said, "Do you still want to marry me?"

He said, "Yes."

When she got off for supper, the two of them went to the courthouse and got a marriage certificate. They went directly to a Presbyterian preacher's house, Horace L. Villee, and got married at 6:55 p.m. Frances' favorite song that year (as well as all her life) was "Melancholy Baby," which would later prove to be prophetic as would some of the others she liked that year, "Goodnite, My Love," "Boo-hoo," "Moonlight and Shadows," "Was It Rain," and "It Looks Like Rain in Cherry Blossom Lane."

Chapter Seven

"If That Diamond Ring Turns Brass . . ."

—Ethel Beatrice Roberts Hatley Rogers (1944)

"Those romantic songs of the 30s," Ethel thought as she looked down at the stunning sight below the plane. The snow-capped mountains were glimmering as though they were iridescent, reminding her of diamonds instead of the gold for which she knew the area was so well known. Glimpses through the clouds on this early morning of June 28, 1944, convinced her that Buck (all the soldiers had nicknames for everything and everybody, so she was calling her husband Buck now all the time like they did) had been dead-on right in his descriptions of the Canadian and Alaskan countryside where he had been stationed for the past year—it was truly spectacular. She wished she could enjoy it a bit more though, but she still felt nauseated from the rough flight. The stewardess had handed her a paper bag when she boarded the plane, but she was so naive she didn't know what it was for. After all, she had hardly been out of the state of Mississippi her whole life. As the plane dipped unexpectedly several times through the turbulence, with its wings moving from side to side, she discovered its purpose. She had taken the early flight at seven a.m. that morning from Edmonton to Whitehorse in the Yukon Territory in Canada on Canadian Pacific Airlines. Her ticket had cost her $97.75.

It was now ll:15 a.m., and she was writing Frances a postcard provided by the airline that showed a stewardess serving a complimentary meal to a grateful passenger who obviously wasn't as airsick as she. She had so much she wanted to tell her only daughter who was living with her husband, Mike (or without him, as the case likely was), now in Mobile at 1164 Baltimore St. She knew Frances was five months pregnant, and she and Buck could expect their second grandchild soon. Judy was just a three-year-old, and here was another one on the way so soon.

Ethel still wasn't sure if she had gotten over the headache she had for months when Frances called that night in November of 1937 and made the announcement.

"Mom, now don't have a fit or anything, but you know that dream of a guy I introduced you to a couple of weeks ago, Mike Sims?"

"Yes, I liked him. What about him?"

"He and I just went off the deep end tonight, I guess. We went to the Presbyterian Church on my supper break and got married! I'm so happy, Mama, and I love him so much. He's the sweetest, squarest guy you'd ever want to know in your whole life. Please say you and Pop will be o.k. with it."

"I guess we'll have to be okay with it. What about Nub though? Does he know?"

"I'll write him a letter. As ya'll have always told me, there's more fish in the sea."

On the plane now, Ethel sighed as she remembered that conversation, which now seemed like eons past instead of a mere seven years. And, as she thought about it now, it had to be okay because everyone knew that once a woman married, she stayed married. She simply had to "stay in the frying pan," as she liked to say, no matter the circumstances.

And the frying pan had been hot for Frances from the very first. Frances had confided to her that she had woken up to life within a week of the "I do's." Mike owed money on a $25 loan at the bank, and Frances had opened up her purse, which contained her drugstore's pay, two and one-half weeks of almost slave labor, and given him the money to pay it back. He stopped by the pool room and used it to shoot craps and came back empty handed. Frances had been furious, but Mike just laughed it off with her and promised that the next time he'd be a winner and would line the bed in which they slept with dollar bills.

Ethel was also thinking about an expression frequently used in the South, "They don't have a pot to pee in," and knew that it described Frances and Mike's situation from the very beginning of their marriage. Mike had gotten a job with a dairy about ten miles south of Clarksdale. Since his aunt and uncle who had raised him had a dairy, he knew everything about cows, horses, and the dairy business in general. A house had been furnished for them, but what a house it was—almost falling down and not a stick of furniture in it. It's a good thing Buck was so well known in the Delta. He went with them to a used furniture store, and they bought on credit what they need-ed to keep house.

There were some good moments, though, for the young couple. Life wasn't entirely bleak for them every day, Ethel knew. Frances couldn't even boil water when she married, but she learned what she had to do to get by. For two years, she fed Mike carrots and kraut and wieners before he told her he didn't like them. The first year Frances continued to think she could be a kid—she played tennis and rode horseback—running home to cook dinner before Mike got home. She even taught Sunday school to the neighborhood kids out in the country where they lived right under the trees every Sunday.

Unlike Nub, Mike was ambitious and likely the best salesman in the Mississippi Delta. As the old saying goes, he could sell "refrigerators to Eskimos" (ironic now, Ethel thought, as she was heading up to Eskimo country for a few months to be with Buck). In the spring of 1938, Mike was offered a job with a bread company making $35 a week, but he and Frances had to move from Clarksdale to Greenwood. They had a two-room apartment close to the hospital, and even there Frances didn't grow up quite yet. One of her good friends and her cousin were in nurses' training there, and the girls would flock to their apartment when their work day was over, sharing the gruesome details of their work.

"And you wouldn't believe the amount of blood that came from that woman after the doctor lanced the boil on her face," Margaret would relate.

Mike was so good at being a salesman, though, that the bread company decided they would use him to get a good route going and then send him somewhere else to do the same. And they were continuing to do what Frances hated most of all—moving constantly. Judy had been born in Gulfport, and now they were in Mobile waiting for the birth of the new baby.

She wanted to give Frances so much advice, but then she remembered Frances had never been open to advice. She always wanted to do everything her way and wouldn't ever listen to anyone, but especially to her and Buck. It was easier through the years just to acquiesce rather than to have a confrontation with her. She also wanted to tell Frances she could always come home if she couldn't make it with Mike. But she couldn't bring herself to write the words. Instead she wrote simply, "Having a wonderful trip. On plane to Whitehorse. Pretty high up. Not afraid tho. 11:15 A.M. Wed. 28th. Wish you'all were along. Beautiful country. I am fine. Love, Mother."

She looked down at her temporary entry record, which had been issued to her two days ago in Emerson, Manitoba. Her address was, 1213 Mississippi Ave. in Greenwood, and here she was, thousands of miles away on her way to visit Capt. John

Wyatt Rogers, her husband of twenty-three years. She had been so proud of him that October 2, 1942, day when he left Memphis for Camp Claiborne, Louisiana, for officers training school. He'd been a part of the 715th Railway Operating Battalion. On the day he went into the Army, they stood by a telephone pole for a photograph. He was in his new uniform, and she was in her gabardine dress. She couldn't take her eyes off him to gaze into the camera; she saw only him.

The men's work in the Army was to be available wherever they were needed and whenever the Army needed railway transportation, principally in the theater of operations. The officers in Buck's battalion consisted of those who were there because of the selective service and from volunteer enlistment of men with railway experience. Since Buck had been with the Illinois Central Railroad since the early twenties, he could go in as a first lieutenant. His job was to be a track supervisor. He had been in the Alaskan-Canadian area (either Skagway or White Horse) since March 10 of last year (almost sixteen months).

From his letters, Ethel knew this past year had been difficult on him. Both of them had anguished over the war, like all Americans had, since the bombing of Pearl Harbor on December 7, 1941, but it was not until Illinois Central started actively recruiting men his age that he thought seriously about volunteering. He had never had any other goal since he knew his work as a newly promoted captain of the 770th Battalion, Co. A, was essential to the war effort, but he was very lonely, and he had missed her terribly, she knew. The Japanese had struck Alaska at Dutch Harbor in 1942, and Ethel knew his work was crucial if the Allies were going to win the war. She had hoped, though, when the "Big Three"—Stalin, Roosevelt, and Churchill—had met in Teheran on the portico of the Russian embassy on December 7, 1943, that peace could come soon. It wasn't to be, however, and Buck was still in Alaska.

His job had been to supervise work on the railroad with his men under him in his battalion on the route from Skagway to Whitehorse. It was one hundred and ten miles long, and the railroad rose from the valley at Skagway, climbing and twisting over mountain terrain to an elevation of 2,900 feet the first nineteen miles.

Along the road were outposts consisting of section houses set beside the tracks. Sometimes, Ethel knew, the men worked as long as thirty-six hours at a stretch without rest and battled the elements that loosened rock slides on their railroad in the summer and snow and ice slides in the winter.

Ethel had clipped an article from the newspaper describing the role of the U.S.O. in making the soldiers' lives a little easier. Jane Hope Whitney (a volunteer for the U.S.O.) described one of her visits as she delivered baked goods, a phonograph, records, books, and mail to them. "At 1:30 one morning last February I got off the train at the first station. Men with lanterns greeted me. Our train had gone through a tunnel of snow that was higher than the top of it. The section house was completely covered with only the chimney showing. The men live in the tunnels they dug from the section house to the small telegraphers' shack. It was like living in an igloo."

Thankfully though, Ethel was going to see Buck during the summertime in the northwestern part of the world. She knew one of the most devastating aspects of soldiers being away from home is their loss of faith in their wives or the girls whom they thought they were going to marry. There were innumerable stories of young wives who decided they wanted someone else after becoming tired of waiting for their soldier husbands. She knew at her age there'd never be anyone for her but Buck, but she had to convince him of that and help if she could to keep up the morale for the other fellows in his company.

She also worried about where he'd be sent once the work at Skagway was complete. The war in the Pacific was accelerating, and she feared he'd be shipped out again but this time to a place where the war was closer and the danger even greater than Alaska. She had lost one husband and a baby son. She had a daughter in an unhappy marriage. She didn't know if she could lose Buck without losing herself also. Going on without him might not be an option for her this time.

Ethel's apprehensions were interrupted by the loudspeaker on the plane, "Ladies and Gentlemen, this is your captain speaking. We are now approaching our landing at Whitehorse. We'll be on the ground in a few short minutes. Weather is . . . "

Ethel could hardly wait to emerge from the plane and was impatient having to wait behind several others. She finally saw

Buck below the steps of the plane at a distance. He came running up to her and hugged her and kissed her. "I can't believe it, darling," he laughed, "Imagine this: The old girl of the sunny south visiting in the frozen north! Who would've ever believed it?"

The next five weeks together were filled with lovemaking and sightseeing in Whitehorse. Indeed she saw sights, as a southern woman, that she never dreamed of. The police were on horses and were known as the Royal Canadian Mounted Police. The Canadian National Park in Prince Rupert was lovely in the summer with new greenery and wildflowers everywhere. She rode on the trail along Deadhorse Gulch and peered over the side of the mountain to see the winding river below and the snow peaks ahead of the tracks (she wrote in her scrapbook, "A trip on this train over this road will make your hair stand up"). She saw dog teams in Dawson and discovered that the Malamute was really more than a dog to the residents in that part of the world. She marveled over the racial diversity and collected postcards of Indians and their children. She walked across the bridge at Miles Canyon on the Yukon River. She picked up a pan containing $15,000 of gold dust on a hot day in July (the 11th). She marveled over the Columbia Icefield Chalet and Athabasca Glacier, she sat beside Lake Bennett, and she was introduced to the legend of Wolf Totem Pole in Prince Rupert. According to legend, one of the ancestors of the man who now owned the pole was disturbed one night by the howling of wolves. He confronted a white wolf who had a sharp piece of deer bone piercing through its jaw. He removed the bone, and man and beast became close friends after that.

On August 5 it was time for her and Buck to spend several weeks in Skagway. She couldn't imagine how their time could be better than it had been in Canada. Even though she was now fifty years old and Buck was forty-seven, it was as if their complete and total love for each other was renewed during this time together, as well as their spirits.

In Skagway Ethel and Buck didn't travel as they had in the Yukon Territory to see any sights; they just had fun together and felt as if they were in their late teens again. They had quiet meals at the Royal Café, which was owned by Mac and Lea Moe and where they could get an exquisite meal of Eggs Vienna for a mere $1.25. She collected autographs and notes from her newfound friends, enticing them to write in her memory book with these words, "Of whom shall we be proud, if not our friends. So honor a page with your name please." Buck, ever the romantic, read to her from his book of poems by northern poets, "There's the gold, and it's haunting and haunting; / It's luring me on as of old; / Yet it isn't the gold that I'm wanting. / So much as just finding the gold. / It's the great, big, broad land 'way up yonder, / It's the forests where silence has lease; / It's the beauty that fills me with wonder, / It's the stillness that fills me with peace."

They laughed together at the legends of Soapy Smith and saw his "skull" there in Skagway on the rock outside of town;

they cried over the orphans at Sheldon Jackson School in Sitka. They loved to tell the story about Ethel's driving the Jeep named "Lillian" so fast that her false teeth went flying out of her mouth onto the road. She wrote on the back of the photo Buck took of her, "How do you like my Jeep? [The picture is] Made in front of the place I live. I have lots of fun riding in this buggy. Wind nearly blows you out at times" and dated it September 1944. They worshipped at the First Presbyterian Church chapel, where Miss Margaret Johnston played the organ and Chaplain A. Mack presented the sermons.

The three months she had in Skagway with Buck had given Ethel the strength that she needed to go forward with the rest of her life, she felt. After she left, he wrote her on November 8, and she could feel once more his extreme loneliness. "darling my dreams of you Have been wonderful, and your stay here was, you will never know how much i enjoyed it, i hope it want be long before we can be to gether again in the good old states... Well, Well. Just Received Your Telegram Of Safe Arrival, And I was In The Midst Of This Letter And The Glad Tiding Of The New Arrival, And Glad to Know that all is Doing So well, give my love to Frances, And The KIDS...Now Grandma Dont you Try to Work Your self in to a frinze Have Much News To Tell You, So I Guess i had bettersign off,...Loving You As Ever All Ways Your Loving Boy, Lots of love and kisses, and a Great Big Hug. My Sweetheart Of Mine, Loveingly Yours, Buck."

Although she would not know it then, two of Ethel's fears

did come true. Buck was shipped out just eighteen days after his letter to her to the Philippine Islands and Korea, where he would serve from August 22, 1945, until December 27, 1945. He would come back into her arms once more, however. Frances would later divorce her husband Mike after thirteen years of marriage. But in the end, Ethel had been able to discover a peace within her that would sustain her through all of her remaining years until her death in 1979. It had begun with the Skagway connection, she was convinced.

Chapter Eight
"Mama's Gonna Buy You a Looking Glass"
—Martha Elise Sims (Lisa) - (1948)

Lisa was staying at her Aunt Elise's and Uncle Dewey's house, which she loved. It was the summer of 1948, and she was three years old. Their house, it seemed to Lisa, was the best house in the whole world. The apartment where she lived with her own Mama and Daddy and Judy was small and unpleasant. Once in her mind she remembered having to get up in the middle of the night.

"Lisa, wake up! Let's put you on the kitchen table for a while." It was Mama talking very slowly what seemed to her like a garbled version of the language. Lisa was yawning and stretching when Daddy picked her up and put her on top of the kitchen table. "What a strange place to be," she was thinking sleepily, but she noticed Judy was already there.

"What are they doing with brooms?" she was thinking as she watched her Mama and Daddy play a game throughout the kitchen and bedroom of the tiny apartment. She had never seen hockey at that time, but the sticks of the brooms were flying comically back and forth—swish, swish. All she could do was to stare above her head as if mesmerized by the single light bulb that hung above the table. She felt tired all over.

Underneath her eyelids, she could hear the voice of her Mama, which sounded very mad. "Darn these rats—darn 'em, darn 'em, darn 'em."

"Just take it easy, Mama, we'll get them, and we'll get a cat tomorrow; you'll see," she heard her Daddy reply with a resigned squeak of an answer as he chased by the table.

At Elise and Dewey's, though, she got to explore the big white house all the time, which her aunt and uncle owned in Webb, and saw nothing scary at all there. There were all the bedrooms down the long hall with the wood floors that were slippery. She could run and slide on them. Her cousin Betty Jean's bed was the one she liked the most of the three since it had a soft feather bed and feather pillows. The bedspread and curtains had pink flowers on them. She liked to sink down into the center of the bed. She felt like a little princess when she took her naps there. Cousin D. P.'s bedroom was boylike—twin beds and chest with a rocking chair. Sometimes Elise would rock her and sing to her like she was still a baby, "Mama's going to buy you a looking glass, And if that looking glass gets broke, Mama's gonna buy you …." Lisa giggled at the funny song and the sound of Elise's broken voice as she sang to her.

Elise and Dewey's bedroom was the biggest, and she liked

going there to listen to the big Philco radio that sat by the wall across from the windows. The kitchen smelled like bananas and coconut, and the dining room had a large table and eight chairs. She was just learning to count and went around and around— "One, two, three, four, five, six, seven, and EIGHT." She finished with a flair in her high-pitched three-year-old voice.

The living room was off limits most of the time, so she only got a peek at it every now and then. She loved the old chairs and sofa, which had hand crocheted doilies on each arm. The large picture on the wall showed a young woman playing a piano. She thought the woman must be Betty Jean.

The hall had some steps leading up to a door in the ceiling. Lisa would never tire of running up and down the stairs every day. She also liked to sit there with her dolls and play, and she wouldn't answer when Elise called her. She liked to hide until Elise was so exasperated that her voice got quivery. Then Lisa'd say in her little voice, "Here I am, Aunt 'Is!"

The front porch was the only cool place on late summer afternoons, and the adults sat out there in their chairs to talk and visit for hours. Sometimes they would all go back to the kitchen and have watermelon. Lisa wore only her panties because of the heat of late August and wouldn't come in until she caught at least two lightening bugs and put them in a jar with holes in the top and a few twigs of grass to make them feel they too were at home.

She wondered where Jute (her nickname for her sister,

Frances

Frances,
Mary Louise,
and
Margaret

The Sims Family

Ethel, Frances, and Slick

Judy and Lisa

Judy, Lisa, David, and Pop

Frances, and Mike

Mom, Frances, and Lisa

Ethel and Slick

Judy and Lisa

Kimberly

Lisa's Wedding

Sheri and Kimberly

Lisa and Kimberly

Family Reunion 1968

Judy) was. Most of the time she was at Elise's with her, but now she looked around, missing her sister. "Aunt 'Is, where is 'Ute?" she asked for yet another time.

"Judy couldn't come this time." Elise explained patiently, "Uncle Dewey and I have just you. Are you having a good time? Your Mama's coming a little while later tonight to see us."

"Uh huh," she replied and ran out to play a few more minutes before the twilight of darkness descended onto the Delta.

Elise had gone into the house to wash the dishes from supper, and Dewey sat in his bedroom with the radio on and a newspaper on his lap. He was nodding his head as if he would fall asleep at any time. The store had been very busy that day, he'd told Elise at supper. He was tired. Daddy Tull was the only one around who seemed to be paying any attention as Lisa would holler out and laugh, "Look at me! Look at me!" for one little trick after another.

Daddy Tull at that time lived not in the main house (as he did after Dewey had his heart attack and died a few years later) but in a little cabin in Elise's back yard. Sometimes Lisa would run around to the back of the big house, streak across the yard on her toes, and take a peek inside. She did that this night.

The door opened easily, and here was the little dollhouse of a cabin before her—almost like the one she had gotten for Christmas from the nice church people who had delivered groceries and toys—except this one didn't have a Mama and Daddy, two perfect children, and a dog named Spot. It had only Daddy

Tull, who had stealthily followed Lisa into his little dollhouse.

"Come here, Lisa," he whispered in a small, strange voice as if he wanted to play a game, "I have a surprise for you." She could see the sweat dripping from his face. He took a handkerchief and wiped it across his forehead.

She laughed and came running into his arms. He started tickling her at first, and she laughed even louder. She could see his khaki pants and his dirty T-shirt and could smell the cigars he smoked all the time. From the corner of her eye, she could see the spittoon he used in his cabin as he sat in his chair and chewed tobacco. It had juice stains on the outside, running down the sides. His stomach was a bit paunchy, and he didn't have a belt on. Holding Lisa with one hand, he used the other to unzip his pants About this time, Lisa started struggling in his arms—not really crying but just trying to slip from his arms so that she could go running back into the kitchen of the big house where Aunt 'Is was.

He turned her over so that her back was against his stomach and bent her over a rail in the cabin that separated the kitchen area from the main room. He pulled down her panties. She began to cry and struggle even more....

Later that night her Mama and Elise had her in the bathtub and were scrubbing her vigorously. It was as if her skin were once again under the collarbone brace she wore after an earlier accident at Aunt Elise's—chaffed and raw. Mama was angry, and Elise was crying. Lisa didn't know what they were saying exactly—their voices were far away and muffled sounding to her as the hot water steamed into the old clawfoot bathtub. "How could you let him? AGAIN. I'm taking her home with me," was all she could interpret her Mama saying that night.

"Good," Lisa thought. "I'll be back home with my 'Ute."

Chapter Nine

"If That Looking Glass Gets Broke,
Mama's Gonna Buy You a Billy Goat"

—Walter Frances Hatley Rogers Sims (1950)

The front door slammed, and unlike Nora in Ibsen's *A Doll's House,* Frances found herself still on the inside of the house. She jumped involuntarily since she didn't know if Mike'd come rumbling back through the door—either to apologize and beg her to take him back yet another time, or to continue to cuss her and throw stuff about the place. She lay in the bed in her two-room apartment at 633 Central with her two girls, Judy and Lisa.

The three of them were sobbing in loud wails interspersed with hiccupy sounds. The girls were crying because she was crying. Frances cried because her heart was as splintered as finely as the old wooden floor in the apartment—which flaked off continually as one walked about on it. She had warned the girls always to have their socks on twenty-four hours a day so they wouldn't get hurt. She needed a sock around her heart, she guessed.

Although her brain was somewhat muddled by the fight

she and Mike had just had, she was still sure she had made the
right decision. She started to think about her situation: "I knew
the day would come when I'd have to leave him—once he started abusing me and the girls."

But knowing the facts in her mind didn't help her to accept
them in her heart. Her heart had been dueling with her mind
since those nights in late September and October of 1937 (with
the full moon and the long walks home from work) when she
had met him. It appeared, though, her mind was finally winning
with a score of 13-0.

It was now almost thirteen years (and two kids) later in the
winter of 1950. She wasn't sure how far back the problems
began with Mike. Could it go back as far as his being raised by
an aunt who seemed to hate him and an uncle who indulged
him? Could it go back to a lack of responsibility for himself
when he got Kizzie pregnant in high school and fathered the
twins, Billy and Bobby?

She knew that their own problems as a married couple had
started practically as soon as they married. She had been so
upset from the beginning that she couldn't even write in her
diary. It had sat on her dresser with several blank days in it
before she could even manage to think about her situation. Not
only had he gambled away the money she gave him to repay his
loan at the bank the first month they were married, but he had
also gotten into serious trouble at the bread company where he
had started to work. She was sure he rationalized it and thought

he would win at craps every time. He had taken the money the customers paid him for bread and gambled that too, losing it of course. He was such a sweet talker, though, that he had talked everyone out of prosecuting him. He'd promise never to do it again, and the two of them would simply go off to another town to start a new route.

Their moves were soon up to fifty-two. She had tried to keep them together since, after a few years, the girls had come along, and she still basically believed that once one married it was forever. In Mobile in 1946, she had finally gotten a job herself; once more Mike was out of one—having spent someone else's money to gamble. They lived in a small house in South Mobile, and the low pay she earned was just enough to feed them. She had to take a bus into North Mobile where her job at the dry cleaners was located. She spent the day (since she had no training for any sort of work) sorting someone else's clothes, bagging them, and checking the buttons.

Judy was five and Lisa not quite two. Judy wasn't in school yet since it was summer, and she had to find a preschool for them to stay. The large house where the nursery was located was downtown and had a big yard for the children to play with toys inside and out. It would be perfect if she could pass the interview. She knew the place was sponsored by the Community Chest of Mobile, essentially some sort of welfare program, but she didn't care. She was desperate and had long ago gotten over her sense of pride about such help.

The basic requirement for every child was that he or she be at least two years old. She remembered taking out Lisa's birth certificate and stealthily changing the date from 1944 back to 1943. She paid $7.50 a week for the two girls, and the county paid the balance.

The three of them had gotten up early every morning, eaten breakfast, dressed, and caught the bus into Mobile. Every day it was a story as familiar and routine as the rising of the sun—she could hear Lisa crying as she took another bus to work. "Mama, Mama," she'd wail for her. Because she was so young though, Lisa soon adjusted and became the darling of the preschool and the school favorite. The staff even made an exception to their age separation rule and allowed Judy to stay in the same group as Lisa. It was easier for them if they didn't have to hear her cry out " 'Ute, 'Ute" all day since Lisa would be unhappy if she couldn't see her sister.

Frances finally decided to move closer to the preschool (only a block away), but what she didn't realize was that it would be moving into a slum area. Her small apartment could accommodate the three of them (and Mike whenever he was around). The kitchen was tiny since it had been made out of a back porch. She had been there just a few nights when she awoke to a huge commotion. The landlady's husband was drunk and had run her and all their children out into the yard of the old house. The kids climbed a big oak tree to get away from him. The police finally came and took him off to jail. Frances had sat on the side of her bed that night (and many others yet to come) praying for her children not to wake up. They never did. When she moved, the landlady came out and said, "Please don't leave, Mrs. Sims, you are the nicest lady we've ever had."

Mike had been in jail during this time and wasn't offering them any help. Frances had pawned her ring to get him out, and he had gone on to Gulfport to see if he could get a job. She had been so embarrassed when her Mama and Daddy had come to see them in the slum apartment. Daddy was still in the Army but on furlough, and they were on their way to Greenwood to see his Mama. They took her to the grocery store and bought her $50 worth of groceries. Daddy had paid for them with a $50 bill, which she looked at with wide eyes—she had never seen one before.

One day when Mike was at home, he decided he wanted to go to Gulfport. He had some business to take care of and thought it would be fun for her and the kids to go along to the beach, together with her cousin Margaret and her four kids. On the way home, about twenty miles out of Mobile, the old second-hand car Mike owned at the time died. They pushed it up to the nearest house and left it. Mike decided they'd all hitch-hike (man, two women, and six young children, two in their mothers' arms). They had walked only a mile and a half when a large black limousine pulled up and offered them a ride. There were two nice gentlemen in front and all of them in the back.

When Mike got the job in Gulfport, she told him she'd follow with the kids if and when he got them an apartment. In less than a week, he called and said he had one, so she packed up again—linens, clothes, a few pots and pans and dishes—and sent everything ahead by railway express. She and the girls caught a bus on Sunday and went over to Gulfport to meet him. He had been so happy to see them, and they had gone out for a nice lunch. Frances asked about the apartment. He just grinned and said, "Well, it's not really an apartment—it's a room, and they don't take children."

He volunteered to take the children to his room, slipping them in a side door, so the three of them could take a nap. Frances got a newspaper and walked five miles before she found a new place to rent. It was a small three-room garage apartment, but it was furnished. The lady owned a dry goods store and the apartment. She listened to Frances' story and loaned her enough household goods to get by on until her boxes arrived. She even took a week's rent instead of the usual month's.

Frances relived her marital experiences in her mind that cold winter's evening, as she lay in bed crying with her girls. She was convinced she would have never left him had he not become physically and verbally abusive to them the past couple of years. She had to let him go. But how could she go on? She would, but she didn't know why—without him. She got out of the bed and put her favorite song on the little record player Mike had bought her:

"Come to me my melancholy baby
Cuddle up and don't be blue

All your fears are foolish fancy, maybe
You know, dear, that I'm in love with you;
Every cloud must have a silver lining
Wait until the sun shines through
Come on and smile, my honey dear,
While I kiss away each tear
Or else I shall be melancholy too . . ."

Chapter Ten
"And If That Billy Goat Don't Pull. . ."
Martha Elise Sims (Lisa) (1960)

The summer of her fifteenth year, Lisa got an opportunity she couldn't resist. One of the lawyers in Tutwiler, whose name was J.W., asked her if she'd like to come into his office on Saturdays and answer the telephone, talk to anyone who might come in, etc. He said he'd pay her $5 a week. In Mississippi in 1960 this amount sounded fantastic to her. She couldn't wait.

By this time she had been living at Mam's house for three years, and it had been the most settled years of her young life. She was finally able to live a normal life. Pop had died suddenly of a heart attack in 1957, and Lisa's Mama thought it would be a good idea for her girls, Judy and Lisa, to live with Mam to give her some company. Mam had never taken care of bills or anything, and Frances reasoned that they could all help one another. Also, Frances herself felt she was on the verge of a nervous breakdown after seven years of waitressing and taking care of kids. She would go to live in Memphis, perhaps even take a business course, and leave the girls with Mam, she reasoned in her mind. The decision would be a benefit for all.

Judy had completed her eleventh-grade year in Greenville and Lisa her seventh-grade year before they moved to Tutwiler. The girls thrived on getting to be children for a while instead of having to take care of their mother so much. With Frances they cooked, cleaned house, shopped, and tried to keep their mother together emotionally. With Mam, they went to ball games with their friends, danced at the community house parties, ran for student council offices, and generally had a good time.

Lisa liked sitting on the front porch by herself at Mam's little white house on the corner of the busy street while Mam watched her soap operas inside. Occasionally, she would glance across the railroad tracks and wonder about the lives of the people who lived over there. As was typical in Mississippi's southern towns, the railroad divided black from white. She saw the Negroes as they sauntered by (happily, it seemed to her) on foot or in their old, noisy cars with mufflers sounding like ascending aircraft. Sometimes a Negro would knock on the door of the house (at the back door, of course) and ask Mam for some food. Mam always had cornbread, meat, and vegetables to share. Or they would come by and ask for handouts of the used *Commercial Appeal* newspapers which Mam read every day and loved. Lisa had no idea what they wanted the old papers for, so she asked Mam about it one day.

"Why, they paper their houses with them," she said, "to

keep the wind out of the cracks when winter comes."

Lisa could remember her visits to Mam and Pop's section house when she was younger and their rides to Greenwood to see Pop's Mama, Miss Polly. One summer afternoon when she was quite young, she was hanging one of Mam's handkerchiefs out the window to be whipped around in the air as she rode along with them in the car, and she heard her grandparents talking of the looming possibility of integration between races.

"Why can't these damn folks stay in their place? Why do they have to stir things up now?" Pop was saying.

His voice was rising higher and higher—enough for Lisa to withdraw her handkerchief from the window and listen more carefully. Since she wanted to join into the conversation with relish, she leaned over the front seat of the car and said, "Well, I'll tell you one thing, Pop, I ain't ever going to school with no niggers!"

"Honey, you just keep talking that way," Pop responded, "and you'll be all right in life."

Obviously pleased with her comment, Pop, along with Mam and Lisa, continued their journey through the Mississippi delta as they had always done.

As she sat on the front porch that day though, Lisa tried to imagine what life would be like for her if she were a Negro. Instead of the little bedroom she and Judy shared in the tiny white house now, she'd have to live in a shotgun house, likely with the beds right there in the front room with the couch, she thought. Her mind drifted momentarily to people of other races in her town and at West Tallahatchie High School. There were no Mexicans, and the only Asian family she knew was there in Tutwiler—the Ben Jue family. He and his wife, Sue, ran a little grocery store where Mam would send her to pick up a loaf of bread, get a popsicle in the summertime, or pick up a watermelon. For her serious grocery shopping, Mam would drive her 1958 Chevy station wagon to Clarksdale, fifteen miles away, to buy from Kroger's. Lisa remembered that Ben and Sue seemed to work awfully hard in their little store. Beyond that, she had no memory. In her classes at school, Lisa had an Indian girl named Essie Mae whom she knew—but didn't know. She spoke to her and all that, but her best friends were Linda, Beverly, Maxine, Mary Jane, Cookie, and Emogene, who were just like her.

When Lisa started her work that summer at J. W.'s office, it seemed as usual that reality didn't match the illusion in her mind. Before she began her job, she imagined that she would be busy all day. She would have an ice-cold Coke at her desk, and she would answer the telephone efficiently and greet those coming into the office with her best smile. It would be a social time for her; she would make money while she was having fun.

Reality, however, was that no one called or came by the livelong day. She was so bored she felt like standing on the desk naked and doing a tap dance. On Saturdays, she decided to entertain herself by reading some of the court cases J. W. had around his office in numerous locations. She chose at random from the bookshelves. Most were as boring as the lack of a ringing telephone or doorbell.

One day though, she picked up a court case and became intrigued by its contents. It was the Emmett Till murder, which took place in Mississippi in her very county just a few years before, in 1955. It read like an exciting novel. She couldn't put it down. She had to keep reminding herself as she read that it was fact, not fiction.

She read that Emmett Till was a Negro boy, fourteen years old, who had come down south for the summer. He was standing around by a general store in Money, Mississippi, there in Tallahatchie County. Evidently, a young white woman came by, and Emmett Till committed the unpardonable sin in Southern society at that time—he wolf-whistled.

As a result of that wolf-whistle and its accompanying fears of mixed race relationships, especially sexual, two white men in the county allegedly took Emmett out into the countryside and brutally murdered him. Lisa's lawyer-employer, J. W., had been one of the defense lawyers when the men were brought to trial.

As she read the court transcript, she became increasingly convinced that these two men were, without a shadow of a doubt, completely and totally guilty of this heinous crime. She had cried when she read the brutal details of the murder. When she turned to the final pages of the document, she was horrified as she read the final verdict from the all-white jury, "Not guilty."

She threw down the transcript and resolved to ask J.W.

about it. She had known him to be a wonderful Christian man at her church, First Baptist. She knew she could trust his views.

Later on that Saturday, J.W. walked in, and the two of them made casual conversation for a few minutes until Lisa could ask him the big question.

"J.W." she began tentatively, "I read the transcript of the Emmett Till trial today, and I wonder how the jury could have possibly found those men not guilty."

J.W.'s demeanor became rigid, and he looked at her as if she had breached some type of sacred trust between them as Southerners. He simply replied, "This is Mississippi."

Later, as Lisa sat on the porch, she remembered the conversation with J.W. in the office; she thought to herself, "If this is really Mississippi, do I want to stay here?" She decided she did not. She determined from that moment that the week after she graduated from high school she would leave the state and never look back. If her life were a novel, this would have been called an epiphany experience.

Chapter Eleven
"Mama's Gonna Buy You a Cart and Bull . . ."
Martha Elise Sims (Lisa) (1961)

It was spring of Lisa's junior year of high school at West Tallahatchie. The past four years had been the best time (and the worst time as those famous first lines go) of her life. For the first time ever, she felt a sense of independence since Judy had gone on to a Southern Baptist college in Clinton and was finishing up her sophomore year. Lisa enjoyed having the tiny front bedroom at Mam's house to herself—at least until Judy came home on vacations, but then she wasn't there very long before she was off to be a counselor at a Girl Scout camp near Jackson. Her Mama was working in Memphis at the Hotel Gayoso. Frances had tried living there with the girls for a while but decided she missed the job that she was best at—waitressing—and had gone back to it. She came back to Tutwiler for visits whenever her work schedule would allow it.

"Shall I, shall I not," Lisa was saying to herself as she sat on the front porch at Mam's and held a flower in her hand

pulling the petals off one by one. It wasn't the possibility of love
that she was thinking about (she wasn't sure that was possible
for her with the betrayals she had experienced from the men
around her, including the middle-aged neighbor across the street
who had been coming over routinely since she was twelve to
paw her when Mam wasn't home). Instead, she was debating
the choice she might make regarding college for herself. On the
one hand, she was smart enough to do the work easily; she made
straight A's, and the other kids would often tease her about never
bringing any books home on the bus to study at night. But then
she thought about truly being independent when she graduated
next spring. She had promised herself after working for J. W. in
his law office on Saturdays that she'd leave the state of
Mississippi the week after she graduated from high school, but
like Mattie in *Ethan Frome,* she continued to ask herself,
"Where will I go?" She wasn't sure.

She knew she had to get away from Tutwiler, however. It
was becoming increasingly difficult to avoid Ernest, the middle-
aged neighbor who lived across the street with his wife, Mary.
He must sit and look out the window to see when Mam drives
away, Lisa thought. She could count on his showing up at the
door on the pretense of giving something to Mam (tomatoes,
squash, etc.) so that she'd have to unlock the screen door to let
him in. It had started when she barely had breasts.

The first time occurred when she was combing her hair
and getting ready to go to a party at the Community House.

Mam had run up to the grocery store to get some milk and bread from Ben Jue's place. She heard knocking on the front door. Mam (and Mama) had always instructed her and Judy never to let anyone in unless they were sure of that person's identity. Lisa knew Ernest, of course. Mary was always over at the house gossiping about everything in Tutwiler and the world in general. Lisa later remembered when Faulkner died in Oxford in July of 1962 that she had come over to announce her opinion of the man. Lisa was reading in the bedroom but could hear every word through the thin walls of Mam's little house.

"Mam, you heard, didn't you, about that old goat William Faulkner dying in Oxford?"

"Now who was he?"

"He's the one who wrote all of those damn nasty stories about the South, that old son of a bitch!"

Mary's husband, Ernest, on the other hand, was no Faulkner, but more like one of the Snopes family. He was overweight by sixty pounds with his pot belly hanging over his pants and continually had a scraggly three-day beard's growth. He and his ancient dog Rex resembled one another with their lumbering walk, panting, and slobbering.

On this particular night, Lisa had thought nothing of unlatching the screen door and letting him come into the house.

"What're you doin?" he questioned.

"Nothing—just getting ready to go to the Community

House."

"Come here and let me look at you."

Lisa came a little closer only to be surprised when Ernest reached out and grabbed her, pulling her close to him. She was evasive, however, and was able to slip out of his grip. She went into the bathroom quickly.

"I'm going to have to go pretty soon; I have to finish getting dressed," she said.

He followed her to the bathroom, and as she stood looking at herself in the mirror, he came in behind her, grabbed her budding breasts with both hands, and began fondling her. His breath was hot, and she could hear him gasping for breath. Again, she took evasive action and wiggled out of his grasp. She went out into the front yard, just as her friend Linda and her parents were pulling up. She got in with them and left while he was standing there looking after the car.

After that night, he seemed always to know when she was alone. She finally confided in Mam, who simply told her to keep the door locked and not answer it when she wasn't there. It seemed like this advice would work at least temporarily, but she was still worried about him several years and several more similar experiences later.

As she thought about college on the front porch, she could see Ernest across the street working in his garden. She shuddered at the memories of his heavy breathing and groping. Yes, she was convincing herself, she needed to move away when she graduated. Her Daddy wasn't making the decision easy, however. Although he had never caused the family anything but anguish, it seemed, for her Mama, Judy, and her, he had written her a letter recently. She pulled it out of her jeans' pocket and read the contents again:

Hello Honey:

I talked to Mam over the phone & she told me about your grades in high school. I am real proud of *Mama's little angel.*

I've got 4 chaps & you are smarter than the other 3 put together & DAD too. Now look how smart you will be i̲f̲ you go to Clinton with Judy for about 4 yr. (4 yr. is not very long).

And a collage degree has a lot of advantages from hear on out.

Now I am not trying to tell you what to do (I guess you hear enough of that). But I think I will have the money for you to go if you want to. See this will be Judy's last year and I just think we can made it O,K. if you want to go.

I want you to write me and tell me what you intend to do so I can try to plan along with it.

I intend to send you another $150.00 on or about 20th of July.

I went to work on this boat the 5th of Aug. (60 days)

Here is a $150.00 just sign my name on the check - (it will be OK)

Write me all the news—and what you intend to do.

I love you & am real proud of you.

Write me soon.

Just,

Daddy

She put the letter back into her jeans' pocket and thought
about his offer. He had let them down so many times before, she
knew, always promising to help out financially and inevitably
failing them. She wondered if she could trust him this time. She
almost hoped he would come through for her.

She looked up the street at the corner of the busy road and
noticed that a man was coming toward their house and was stag-
gering from one side of the street to the other. She hoped it was-
n't who she thought it might be. As he got closer, she stood up
and peered through the screen. She recognized her Daddy.

"Hey, little Widget, how you been? Honey. . ." he slurred
his words, "I need you to carry me to Clarksdale . . . to see a
man about a job."

"I don't know," Lisa stalled. "I'll have to ask Mam if she'll
let me borrow the car."

She was feeling rather resentful that he had just written her
promising to help financially if she chose to go to college, and
now here he was at their door, drunk and probably broke again as
usual . She hoped none of her friends like Bobby or Melvin drove
by and saw him there at her house. She was ashamed of him.

"I'm not sure I can do that right now," she said with her
voice rising and becoming edgy.

By this time Mam had heard the commotion and came out

of the kitchen drying her hands on a dish towel. "Hey, Mike, I thought I heard you out here."

"Mrs. Rogers, tell . . . Miss Astor here. . . that she can drive me to Clarksdale," he slurred again.

"I DON'T WANT TO DRIVE YOU TO CLARKS-DALE. CAN'T YOU UNDERSTAND THAT?"

"What do you think I'm going to do. . . RAPE YOU?"

By this time, Lisa had burst into instantaneous tears. Mam was angrier than Lisa had ever seen her in her sixty-seven years of life. "Mike, you ought to be ashamed of yourself—talking to your own daughter that way. I'll take you where you need to go. Get in the car right now!"

After they left, Lisa felt drained and energyless. She lay on her twin bed and put on her Nat King Cole 45 rpm record of "Mona Lisa":

"Do you smile to tempt a lover, Mona Lisa?

Or is this your way to hide a broken heart?

Many dreams have been brought to your doorstep

They just lie there and they die there

Are you warm, are you real, Mona Lisa?

Or just a cold and lonely lovely work of art?"

Yes, she thought to herself, "Maybe the best thing to do is to leave this state the week after I graduate after all."

Chapter Twelve
"And If That Cart and Bull Fall Over . . ."
Walter Frances Hatley Rogers Sims (1961)

Frances once again lay in bed pondering her options. "Should I marry Nelson or not?" she asked herself over and over again. It was the summer of 1961, and she was as close to a nervous breakdown as she would ever get. She often told Judy and Lisa that she could not even stand to see her old friends on the street; she would simply hide to avoid speaking to them. The plan for Lisa and her, though, had sounded like, once again, a perfect one in her mind. She and Lisa would go down to the Mississippi coast the way they always had in the summer. Judy was a camp counselor at a Girl Scout camp near Jackson, and Mam would get a bit of a break from Lisa. Lisa was becoming somewhat wild, according to Mam, riding up and down the road with Bobby on his motorcycle or Melvin in his little Austin Healey Sprite. Both of them worried about her choice of friends as well as her safety. Maybe she could be a positive influence on her daughter.

"Some time with you, Frances, would be good for her,"
Mam had convinced her. "You can work on your relationship
together."

As usual, they had taken off, like the mother and daughter in
Anywhere But Here, with neither having a job. Lisa was sixteen
and could now legally work. Frances thought maybe a carhop's
job would be just the thing for her—give her a little responsibility.
She herself would work somewhere there on the gulf—maybe at
the Holiday Inn Restaurant again. But once the two arrived on the
coast, life there did not go as well as she had hoped.

When they arrived, Frances woke up every day feeling
exhausted, as if she couldn't put one foot in front of the other.
She was so thankful, though, that they had been able to rent
Mrs. Estes' upstairs apartment again right there across from the
beach in Gulfport and just a short walk to the municipal pier.
Lisa was working every day from four until midnight a couple
of houses down from them at a little drive-in called Pam's.
Frances had managed to work a couple of weeks herself before
the anxiety and depression became too much for her to endure.
Then one day she found she simply couldn't get out of the bed.
She wasn't quite like Gregor in *The Metamorphosis;* she didn't
fancy herself turning into a giant beetle, but she couldn't func-
tion normally anymore. She considered her options, as best as
her mind would allow, and thought about what to do. Lisa did-
n't understand her at all.

"You're supposed to be the mother," Lisa's voice was loud

and panicky, "You're supposed to take care of me, not the other way around."

"I just can't right now," Frances cried. "I don't know what we're going to do. Our money's running out. I've written your daddy for help, but I haven't gotten anything yet."

After Lisa went to work at Pam's that day, Frances tried to analyze how she had gotten from point A to point B. It wasn't like she hadn't had lots of opportunities to get married again since she and Mike divorced in 1950. She just wanted to make sure that the girls got a good stepfather like Pop had been for her. As she thought about her serious (and not so serious) boyfriends of the past, she realized that she had six. The very first memory she had was of Hank, whom she had met in Azar's in Greenville shortly after her divorce was final.

She had been so much in love with him. He was an Indian from Oklahoma who had come to work as a crop duster in the Mississippi Delta. She worried about his job, but he always assured her that his eyes were better than 20/20 and he couldn't imagine ever doing anything else. One night he had proposed to her.

"Frances, I think we could make a good team together," he said, "Do you want to go ahead and marry me?"

She thought about his relationship with his first wife and the dreaded fact—he had never gotten over her. Frances had to ask him.

"Hank, do you love me? I know you'd be good to Judy and Lisa, but do you love me?"

"I care for you. I need someone in my life," he replied.

"But you don't love me, do you?" she persisted.

"No, I have to be honest with you. I still love my first wife," he replied.

Shortly after that, he returned to Oklahoma.

Her next couple of boyfriends really weren't that serious. There was Harry, who took them for rides across the Mississippi River every Sunday afternoon, but frankly, she worried about his influence on the girls. For example, on one of the Sunday drives, he had shown Judy and Lisa how to take a check that had been made out for $3 and change it effortlessly to read $300. Both the Arabic number and the cursive description on the forged check looked authentic. The girls had been greatly impressed, but she began to worry about the man she thought she knew well but perhaps didn't.

Joe was the next boyfriend, who was a mere twenty-eight years old to her thirty-seven. He was an airman at Keesler Air Force Base there in Greenville. She had such fun with him. His blond hair and broad smile were infectious. She always felt that he cared more about the girls than her and he just missed his family back home. She remembered how he helped her plan Lisa's eleventh birthday party at the Indian Mounds. It was to be a cookout and a joint celebration with Shirley, a girlfriend, who was born the day after Lisa had been born—same hospital in Clarksdale (Frances often teased Lisa that Shirley was more like her than Lisa was; perhaps there had been a hospital mix-up). When Joe got stationed at another base, they kept in touch for a while but then she didn't hear from him again. He had been so close to all of them; morbidly she brooded that something had happened to him and that no one would know to call her.

Doyle was next. He was a paraplegic. He had been in a wheelchair for years, but when he proposed, she seriously considered marrying him. She even went to his physician and asked about the sexual part of the marriage and how all that would work—if it could work. After one difficult marriage, however, she decided she didn't have the courage, and certainly not the energy, to assume the responsibility for his physical care.

Ronnie and she had met on the coast one year instead of in Greenville. He was working for Holiday Inn just like she was. He was laying carpet for them, and she was waitressing. He was a short, red-haired guy with a fantastic sense of humor; they always had such fun together. She had never been with anyone since Mike who was so totally carefree, it seemed. Even when money ran tight that summer (Holiday Inn was a bit tardy sending him his money for the completed job), he kept them laughing while they waited on it. Every night he'd come to the upstairs apartment at Mrs. Estes', and the four of them would eat red beans and rice. It was cheap, and it had a lot of protein.

Finally, the check came. It was for $90. Frances remembered the scene they made in front of the girls, hugging and laughing and talking about going to the grocery store. As the four of them walked through the grocery aisles, it was like

Christmas for them. At one point, Lisa asked tentatively, "Can I have some green grapes?"

"Yes, honey," Ronnie had replied, "We're in the money finally; you can have anything in this store you want!"

The trouble was that Ronnie still had a wife and a young son, and he wasn't ready to leave them. He said frankly to her that he couldn't leave them.

Frances had thought she would never love anyone after Hank, but she found romance again quickly and in the workplace once more. She had gotten a job for a brief few weeks right after Pop died in 1957 at the cotton compress in Clarksdale. M.H. also worked there. They were instantly attracted to one another, and M.H. promised to teach her something she had never learned to do—drive a car. After work, they'd go out and drive on the country roads together. She was extremely nervous about learning how. The car would weave and buck, and he'd be sitting beside her laughing. "You can do it, baby. You can do it," he'd coax.

Like Ronnie though, M.H. also had a wife and two kids. Tutwiler was a small town, and Frances worried about the inevitable gossip—especially from Mary across the street if she discovered anything. One hot night when Mama and Judy were gone and Lisa was in the bedroom, they had the inevitable argument.

"I can't let you do it, M.H. I can't let my girls be subject to the gossip that would happen if you divorced and we married. I've always done everything within my power to make sure they had a good life."

"But I love you so much," M.H. pleaded.

In a couple of weeks, Frances pulled up stakes once again and moved to Memphis on the pretense that she missed the job she was best at—waitressing. Only she (and Lisa) knew the real reason she left the girls at Mama's.

When Lisa called her a few weeks later to tell her that M.H. had died suddenly that morning of a heart attack, Frances felt she couldn't breathe as she was hearing the news. She had just talked to him on the phone the night before, and he was pleading with her once again to come home and marry him. He was just in his forties. She was distraught and felt responsible somehow.

Every day she made herself go to the Hotel Gayoso and work her two jobs—at noon she was hostess and at night she waitressed. She lived in a room with a family she had met in Lake Cormarant when she was a child. She put one foot in front of the other to keep going, but she knew she was existing only, not living.

One night as she was coming through the hotel lobby to her job, she saw a couple of people from a distance who seemed to be staring at her.

"Frances, is that you?" the woman called before she even got close.

"It's Lois." Frances' mind instantly went back to her high school days in Lambert when she and Lois were best friends. Both of their fathers had worked for the railroad, and Frances ate Mrs. Freeman's good food all the time.

"You remember Nelson, don't you?" Lois was saying as he extended his hand.

"I guess I've changed some since I've seen you," he laughed, remembering that he had a crush on her when he was thirteen and she was sixteen. She hardly knew he was alive back then with Bruce and Nub and all the others who were rushing her for attention. Now she paid attention. He was tall, had dark hair, wore glasses and had thick (what seemed to her to be painted on) eyebrows—still rather strange looking, she thought, but he seemed nice.

Nelson was taking courses at a business college and hoped to get a job as an engineer in industry. He also had a family—a wife, Avis, and a daughter, Elaine, back home in Isola. Even though he wasn't her idea of an extremely handsome man like Mike, he had a remarkable capacity for listening. She talked for hours with him that night after work and many others in the days to come. He made it a habit to eat there in the restaurant, and then he'd make sure she got back to her room safely. She told him about M.H. and the pain and hurt she was still experiencing. He didn't judge her actions at all. He accepted her just like she was—unconditionally. She liked that.

When he suggested that he was going to divorce Avis and would like to marry her, Frances felt the same fear that she had with M.H. She worried about her girls, but then who would really know the circumstances, since they lived in Memphis? She told him she'd take the summer off, take Lisa to the coast, and think about it. She'd give him an answer soon.

She had been close to a nervous breakdown once before when her daddy had died. She found then—as now—she could hardly look at anyone or talk to anyone anymore. She would cross the street to avoid having to stop and make small talk, even with the people she had known for years. Now she felt that same sense of anxiety and powerlessness. She was beyond functioning. She would pick up the phone and tell Nelson yes. With the waiting time for divorces, she knew they could be married by the new year—1962.

Chapter Thirteen
"Mama's Gonna Buy You a Dog Named Rover"
Martha Elise Sims (Lisa) (1962)

Lisa kept her promise to herself that day she was working for J. W. in the lawyer's office, and left Mam's house the week after she graduated from high school at West Tallahatchie. Frances and Nelson had been married six months by that time and were living in Wichita, Kansas. She looked forward to a new life in a new state, but she felt a bit lonely. Judy was back with her high school boyfriend, Bobby, and their relationship looked serious this time—unlike their high school dating experience, which ended when Judy announced she wanted to stay a virgin, until she married. Bobby was back now and evidently content to wait until marriage for the consummation of their relationship. Judy was going into her senior year at Mississippi College, and this summer she would be counseling at a Girl Scout camp in rural Kansas, about ninety miles from Wichita. Her Mama had Nelson, and thankfully so, since she had come down in the spring of 1962 with a mysterious illness. It seemed to be similar to pneumonia, but the doctors could never diagnose it for certain. It had kept her from attending Lisa's graduation, and as usual, Lisa thought it was all about her.

"She can't come to my graduation. She's never been there when I needed her!" Lisa wailed to her current boyfriend, John E.

"I'm sorry, baby. If I could change things for you I would," he tried to comfort her.

Lisa had considered marrying John E. her senior year, but she felt she wanted more from life than simply scraping by. John E.'s dad was barely more than a sharecropper in the delta, and John E. had struggled hard to complete his credits for high school graduation. He often had to miss a lot of school days to help his daddy out on the farm, drive the tractor, and pick cotton. He seemed to love her though and was very supportive in their senior year experience of being boyfriend and girlfriend. In February they had been nominated for Mr. and Mrs. West Tallahatchie High School. On February 28 when her business education teacher, Miss Meyers, read the names of the winners from the announcement sheet, Lisa had mixed emotions. She had won the honor, but John E. had not. As she thought about her options after graduation, Lisa knew that if she went to Wichita and it didn't work out with a job and living with her mother and Nelson, John E. would be waiting for her. It could still be a win-win situation.

The trip to Wichita had been a long and tiring one. Judy sat in the front seat with Nelson, and Lisa in the back seat.

Nelson, in his nervousness perhaps to make a good impression on them, talked incessantly.

"And the B-24 took off from base at eight in the morning. We were on a reconnaissance mission to take out the targets at..." Nelson droned on and on.

By two in the afternoon, they stopped at a small filling station in Missouri. In the filthy bathroom, Judy started begging.

"Please, Lisa, sit in the front seat for a while with Nelson. I'm so sleepy I can't hold my eyes open," she pleaded.

"No way in the world I'm gonna do that," was Lisa's only response.

In Wichita, their Mama was still in the bed, trying to get well but not responding well to the antibiotics. Periodically, she would have to be re-hospitalized, have fluid drawn from her lungs, and returned home again. Judy went on to camp, and Lisa set about trying to find a job. She had taken typing, shorthand, and bookkeeping her senior year and hoped these skills would at least get her a receptionist's or a secretary's job.

Her Mama and Nelson had joined Immanuel Baptist Church in Wichita, and Lisa attended with them (whenever her Mama felt like going). On the first Sunday Lisa went into the sanctuary, she wore a backless, polished cotton yellow dress Mam had made for her before she left. She had on matching yellow heels. With her tan, she thought she looked great. As the service began, she noticed one of the ushers in the service. He was a young man with blond hair and a warm, wide smile. She thought she might like to get to know him. She also had her eyes on another guy in the choir with blonde hair.

In a week or so, she decided to attend Baptist Training Union one night before the evening church service. She was the first one in the room, but soon a young man came in. He was the usher she had been watching in the church service.

"Hi, my name's Garlan," he introduced himself. In a few short minutes, Lisa learned he was twenty-two years old and worked as a delicatessen manager for one of the grocery chains in the city, Mr. D's. He always volunteered to cater the food for events that the youth were having in the church.

They talked for a while longer before the activities for the hour started. As they were all leaving, Garlan came up to Lisa's side and walked out with her. "Do you think we could do something together this next weekend? Maybe we could go out on Friday night and have dinner and then on Saturday night we could go to a movie," he suggested. Lisa had never been asked for two dates at once and was impressed. She eagerly accepted his offer.

It was not until they had been married thirty years that Garlan's mother told her the story of a mother's prayer.

"You know, Lisa, when Garlan was in his early twenties, all of his friends were getting married. He was groomsman in so many weddings it seemed—always the attendant and never the groom. He came to me one day and said, 'You know, Mom,

I don't know if I'll ever find anyone for myself." I told him not to worry—that the right girl would come along if he'd just be patient. From that moment on, I began to pray for my son's wife—that just the right one for him would come along. It was shortly after that you moved to Wichita from Mississippi and he met you . . ."

Chapter Fourteen
"And If That Dog Named Rover Don't Bark..."
Kimberly Michelle Brandom (1971 and following)

"The red ones, I 'ant the red ones, Mama!" three-year-old Kimberly hollered at her mother on a crisp fall morning in 1971. The Brandom family was getting ready for church in Ruleville, Mississippi,where they had been living for a year and a half.

"But, Kimberly, don't you think these cute little black Sunday shoes would look better with your dress that MeMa made you?" coaxed Lisa.

"I 'ant the red cowboy boots!" Kimberly again yelled and began pulling off the black shoes her Mama had already put on her feet. Her back began to arch from the small chair she was sitting in. Her feet were flailing out in rapid movements to keep at bay any resistance that her Mama might offer to her own plans. "I like the red ones best!"

Her mother sighed and knew the battle was lost in light of the time. "Why is it," Lisa wondered to herself, "that things can go relatively smoothly until it's Sunday morning and we're rushed?"

Lisa had known motherhood was going to have its chal-
lenges, and she had prepared for them by reading for hours in
Dr. Spock's *The Common Sense Book of Baby and Child Care.*
He seemed to have an answer for strong-willed children like her
daughter. She'd reread that section again, she told herself, after
church and dinner today.

"Kimberly certainly came into this world with a mind of her
own," thought Lisa with a smile as she thought about the preg-
nancy books she had also read from the first month. According to
them, first babies came after a long and hard labor, sometimes
up to twenty-four hours. Kimberly, however, had other plans, it
seemed. She came quickly on the morning of October 3, a mere
one day after the due date. Lisa had gotten up around three a.m.
after experiencing mild cramping pains and sat for almost three
hours reading the symptoms of labor over and over again. When
the pains got so strong, at six a.m., she didn't need to read any
longer but quickly awakened Garlan. They were just a couple of
minutes away from Lafayette County Hospital in Oxford—which
was good—since Kimberly arrived shortly before eight a.m.

From the very beginning, Kimberly wanted to let her parents know that she was in control, not they. Since this was the
first child for her parents to practice on, she was pampered and
rocked in her chair (a present from Mam, her great-grandmoth-
er). From the beginning she never liked food very much and
was indifferent to both nursing and then later to eating cereal

and baby food.

"Please, Kimberly," Lisa would gently coax, "just eat two bites of green beans."

Lisa would often hide the vegetables and meat at the back of the spoon behind the peaches or pears. Sometimes it would go down, and sometimes Kimberly would spit out the whole spoonful onto her chin.

Dr. Spock didn't get upset in his book about these little adjustment problems, so why should Lisa and Garlan, they told themselves? It was a bit difficult, however, to get enough sleep since they were then full-time students at the University of Mississippi. Garlan would crawl into bed, thinking baby Kimberly was sound asleep, only for both of them to be awakened within the next minute or so by a loud, piercing wail. Lisa would then get up and take her turn at the rocking chair with their daughter.

At eight months, Lisa's sister, Judy, came for a visit. "You'll just have to let her cry it out if ya'll are ever going to get a full night's sleep again," she said confidently, since she was already the mother of two, Faith and Bruce.

"I don't know; it seems so cruel for us to let her cry like that."

After a particularly difficult time one night about two a.m., Lisa and Garlan decided to close the door to her room and try the crying time. After wailing for thirty minutes or so and standing at the foot of her bed, she fell over backward and slept the rest of the night. Lisa and Garlan were relieved to have won that battle.

By the time the Brandom family had moved to Springdale, Arkansas, in 1972, Kimberly was on her way to being a near-perfect child. Every once in a while, though, she would slip into her old independent ways again of babyhood through three years. When she was five, and her baby brother, Chris, was one, her Mama fell and sprained her ankle. She lay on the sofa with her crutches by her side and took care of Chris while Kimberly rode her big wheel outside in the driveway. She could hear her daughter through the storm door making her roaring sounds like a male truck driver. She knew the rules: Never ride the big wheel out of the driveway. Lisa didn't worry; Chris was asleep in his bedroom. Lisa began to feel sleepy from the pain medication the doctor had given her. The phone started to ring, and it took several rings for Lisa to get to it with the hobbling.

"Lisa," one of the neighbor's voices was on the other end of the line, "did you know Kimberly is riding down the street by herself alone on her tricycle?"

"Heavens, no," Lisa began to feel panicky and felt fear pulse throughout her body. "I've sprained my ankle and can't get to her. Would you please go out and bring her home? Thanks so much."

Lisa had always prided herself on watching her children very closely and taking care of their every need. In fact, one of her close friends, Judy, had been critical lately, "Why do you do everything for those kids? Kimberly can open the car door for herself now; why don't you let her do more for herself?"

she questioned.

Lisa was imagining that Kimberly might get her hand caught in the car door if she allowed her to be so independent. She also remembered occasionally all that had happened to her as a child when someone wasn't watching her closely—sexual abuse, a broken collarbone, and other traumas.

"No," Lisa thought, "I can't let her do that just yet."

The doorbell rang, and Kimberly was there with the neighbor who had called. After the lady left, Lisa burst into tears. "Kimberly, why did you disobey me? You know you're not to ride the big wheel out of the drive?" The thought that Lisa had lost control of her daughter for just a few minutes was overwhelming to her.

Kimberly started crying also; as everyone knows, daughters always cry when their Mamas do. It was another step toward independence, though, for Kimberly from her Mama. She felt a little proud of herself that she had been so brave. She had an adventure, although a short one.

Lessons for Kimberly came primarily through her Mama who was always on duty, it seemed, for rules and tact lessons. "Kimberly, it's probably not the most tactful thing you did this afternoon in the car when you told Helen that you had called about ten other people to go to the movie with you before anyone accepted."

"Why, what's wrong with that?" Kimberly inquired.

By the time she was in the sixth grade, Kimberly had perfected her tact and could abide by her Mama's rules, but she had another voice speaking to her as well—God's. It seemed to her that she had always been a Christian since, from the very beginning of her memories, she had gone to First Baptist in Springdale with her family. When she was five years old, she remembered going forward in the old Barnhill Arena when James Robison, the evangelist, was in Fayetteville for a spiritual crusade. She considered herself to be a Christian from that moment on and never had any doubts about her salvation. She postponed, on her Mama's advice, getting baptized officially in the church until she was in the third grade—on Christmas Day— because Mama had said that would be a wonderful Christmas present for her.

When Kimberly was going into her seventh-grade year, she had come to the peak, she thought, of her athletic abilities thus far. She had played softball since she was a third grader, with her long blonde hair down to her waist and her baseball cap and team shirt on. She was the pitcher for the team and knew without a doubt that she was the best player. It was a warm summer evening, and she was feeling quite proud of her leadership and contribution to the team.

"Come on, Kimberly, get a hit!" the other girls were yelling. "You can do it!"

Kimberly felt the crack of the bat and the sound it made when the ball hit the sweet spot of the bat. She was also the fastest runner on the team. She'd make at least to second base, she thought to herself.

As she was rounding first on the way to second, she heard a crack in her left knee. She made it safely to second base, but she knew something was very wrong. She managed to hobble around until the end of the game. Her Mama was home; she'd know what to do. Mama was fixing supper when Kimberly and Garlan came in. When Kimberly couldn't eat any supper, and sniffled throughout the meal, Mama insisted that Garlan take her to the emergency room for an x-ray. After being gone several hours, they came home once again—this time Kimberly had a cast on from her upper thigh to her foot. She had cracked her kneecap. As she thought about it later, Kimberly believed that pride had literally caused a fall in her case, and she realized that God often taught humility in surprising ways.

When Kimberly was sixteen, she was once again a top athlete and scholar in her small Christian school, Shiloh. She ran the two-mile event in track and had just won the honor of going to state for competition. She also played basketball and had a lot of good games shooting her three-point shot. It was the best school year of her life, she thought, primarily because she was free and independent. Her Mama had taken a new job that year at a nearby university as an adjunct in the English department, which meant she was no longer hovering over her and controlling her every move.

She still paid attention, however, to Mama's advice. When she ran for the office of vice president for her senior class the next year, Mama had suggested she read Rudyard Kipling's famous poem, "If." Even though her Mama knew it was a cliché, she felt it would be right for this audience.

"I don't know, Mama," Kimberly hedged as she was making notes for the speech, "I don't know that anything can move this bunch of juniors."

"Just try it for me, Kimberly. I think they'll like it."

"O.K. I'll end with it maybe."

Awards day was also coming up, and Kimberly didn't know if she'd win any awards, but she hoped she would. When the day arrived, it was as if Kimberly created a constant breeze, since she was walking up to the podium so frequently to receive award after award. She was sorry her Mama couldn't be there, but she was in Texas with Judy for a family event. She was so thrilled with the attention but longed for her Mama to hear the news—about the many awards, of course, but especially the fact that she had been elected as the new vice president, because it was recognition from her peers.

"You were right, Mama," Kimberly said to her mother in Texas, "I didn't think this class could be moved, but they all thought it was a wonderful speech!"

Chapter Fifteen

"Mama's Gonna Buy You a Horse and Cart"

Walter Frances Hatley Rogers Sims Freeman (1979)

Frances stood by herself on the deck of the Sun Princess as it cruised northward toward her destination of Alaska. It was fairly early for her, eight a.m. She knew that Nelson was back in the cabin getting dressed for the day. She already felt as if she had been treated like Mrs. Astor since they had just had breakfast, and it had been delivered directly to their cabin this morning. She was thrilled with the efficient service by the ship's staff.

Her thoughts began to drift backward in time like a boat unloosed from its mooring. She thought about her Mama and the experiences she must have had in Alaska in the 1940s. Now, as she remembered Mama's dependence on Pop for her every need, she couldn't believe that her own mother had been brave enough to tackle such a trip on her own. She had actually gone to Chicago and boarded an Illinois Central train for a large part of the trip and had flown on from Edmonton, Canada, to Whitehorse in the Yukon territory. Up until that time, her Mama had never flown.

Frances smiled as she felt the Arctic wind on her face on this late September morning in 1979. Mama had been dead since January and had spent the last six months of her life in a nursing home in Springdale, Arkansas, where Lisa and Garlan had been able to see her every day and take care of her needs and bills. She wondered why mother-daughter relationships always seemed to be so problematic. As she recalled her early life, it seemed that she and Mama had gotten along fairly well. After all, her Mama and Pop doted on her and spoiled her terribly. She knew that now. Their relationship seemed to fall apart though when she married Mike so quickly in 1937 and almost literally left her childhood sweetheart, Nub, standing at the altar.

As usual with Mama, she could never have a serious discussion with her. She longed to tell her Mama that she had made a serious mistake by marrying Mike. She imagined the conversation to have gone like this:

"You know, Mama, you were right the first few years when you worried that Mike and I weren't going to make it as a couple."

"So, Miss Frances, you can finally see that now, can you?"

"Yes, the thing that I wish most, though, is that you and Pop had come to rescue me from the situation I was in. Ya'll must have known that we lived in squalor most of the time. Why didn't you come for us and take us home with you?"

"Well, I think it was because we believed deep down that you had made your bed and you needed to sleep in it. We didn't want to interfere."

Instead, however, she and Mama never spoke of it directly. There was an uneasy peace between them as long as Pop was alive. When he died and Frances suggested that she and the girls move in with Mama, their relationship deteriorated even more.

Frances tried living in that small town, but after being independent and on her own with the girls for seven years already in Greenville (a much larger town of 40,000), she knew the first month or so that it wasn't going to work. She and Mama argued over everything: whether or not to lease the local restaurant, how to cook the meals (certainly not on the highest heat), and what school clothes Lisa and Judy needed.

Soon she was off to Memphis on the pretense of being able to make more money back in the restaurant business so that Judy could go to school at Mississippi College, a private institution. The real reasons were that Mama was driving her crazy, and M. H., her married lover, was urging her to marry him if he could get a divorce from his second wife.

When Mama had to go into the nursing home last year, Frances had been totally unable to assist the girls in getting a place for her and helping Mama in her adjustment to living in a health care center. She had gone down from Seattle, she thought, to help, but had fallen apart when they took Mama into the front door. She could hear Mama's voice pleading, "Frances, I know what you're doing. You ought to be ashamed of yourself for doing this to your own Mama." It seemed she cried for days after she got back to Nelson in Seattle.

Frances' mind now drifted over to Mike. Had the marriage really been this huge mistake that everyone else in the world thought it was? She often said that, while he was sober, no one could have ever asked for a squarer, nicer, more loving man. He had the best sense of humor of anyone she had ever known, and that was important to her; God knows she needed those memories when times later got tougher between them. She experienced the worst day of her life (and his first wife, Kizzie, said the same thing) on Mike's funeral day in August of 1976. Even though she had always expected his life would end tragically, and she had always insisted that he carry identification on him while they were together, she never thought he'd be shot to death. She didn't know if she could ever get over him (she loved him deeply still and always would).

Yet as she stood on the deck that morning, she was grateful that Nelson had provided the moorings for her for the past twenty years. He had been there listening and comforting her through the sudden death of M.H. right after she moved to Memphis, and he had been there for her during the deaths and her recovery from her grief (if one ever did truly recover) for Mama and Mike. As an avid lover of crossword puzzles all her life, she knew the alternate definition of the word *moorings;* he truly had been the element providing stability and security for her grief. It wasn't as if God weren't there for her too, she thought, but God provides significant others to listen as well.

"Passengers, it is now time for the nondenominational church service in the chapel," the purser announced over the intercom. Frances quickly went inside where she was to meet Nelson. There was a large crowd of people, and the service was inspirational with seemingly heartfelt prayers offered up to God for His goodness and the beauty of the world He had created.

On the next day, as the ship was being steered more and more north, she and Nelson saw their first whale on the trip and icebergs for the first time. She had the same feeling Mama must have also had in the 1940s, total exhilaration, since they were both Southern women going to the frozen North. As they docked in Juneau about two p.m., they were both entranced by the town, which was scattered over the mountains and waterfront. They quickly signed up for a tour to Mendenhall Glacier, and they were soon drinking coffee (milk for Nelson) in the towering lodge with its accompanying fireplace that faced the glacier, separated only by clear glass. They drove to the chapel on the lake, where they could get an even better view of the glacier. The building also had a huge window from which they could see the glacier being framed by the gigantic beams within the chapel forming a cross. She knew she had never felt so close to God than at that moment—or to her husband.

On Tuesday Frances' heart was like a bouncing ball. This was the day she had been waiting on—on this day the travel agenda indicated that she and Nelson (and all the cruise passengers) would be docking in Skagway. She stepped off the ship at eight a.m. and saw the 1880s town with its boardwalks and little shops. The snow-peaked mountains were surrounding the town and had just received their second snow of the season, according to the locals. More than anything, she wanted to find the house where Mama and Pop had lived during the war. They walked around town but couldn't locate it.

It was time for the bus trip to Whitehorse in the Yukon Territory. As the bus slowly ascended the mountain to the top of White Pass, the sun broke through the clouds and fog to reveal the gold of the aspen trees, which were at their peak of color. They drove into Carcross, a stopover for many of the gold miners during the Gold Rush days in the late 1800s. Driver Pat Price told them story after story, many of which centered on the antics of a local character named Soapy Smith, who owned a "parlor" in Skagway and was a con man.

They were back on the ship too soon, but the next day was the Glacier Bay experience. Both she and Nelson held their breath as the ship came within one-fourth of a mile from John Hopkins Glacier, comparable to a building more than twenty stories high. Pieces of it broke off repeatedly, sounding like explosions. The scenery was so awe-inspiring that the captain ordered a brunch to be set up outside. Part of the crew was even dispatched to retrieve pieces of the glacier to chill the wine for dinner. Frances thought they truly were in a land of mystery, so unlike the lower 48; even the glacier ice had a strange and unearthly texture.

The final night aboard the ship featured a captain's farewell party with decorations of red, white and blue—delicious steak fillets and what else but baked Alaska were served. The strolling violinist and the accordion players stopped at their table to play Frances' favorite song, "Melancholy Baby," for her. She took Nelson's hand since she knew it had been requested especially for her. Life was finally good, she thought.

Chapter Sixteen
"And If That Horse and Cart Breaks Down,"
—Kimberly Michelle Brandom (1992)

The only trouble was that this was her Mama's dream for her, not her own. It was spring of 1992, and Kimberly lay in the bathtub reviewing her options regarding her life and graduate school. She had been in Los Angeles for three years now at the University of Southern California and had progressed rapidly through her master's degree in English, completing it in a mere three semesters and a summer. She went on for her Ph.D. and had recently been declared officially an A.B.D. student (all but dissertation). The language exam in German hadn't been as hard as she thought it might be, and the comprehensives, even though they were all grueling, she had also passed with flying colors.

She had found academic life, however, to be totally pedantic. It seemed, with the exception of her good friends, Madja and Walt, that most of the students in the program were so full of themselves and their intellect (which they loved to show off in class). While the profs were definitely the top of the field of

English, they too wrote and spoke in a language that was at best barely understandable. Their rhetoric and vocabulary were so filled with statements like, "The signifier is an arbitrary descriptor for the signified," that her head spun at times simply to understand their lectures. She thought this extremely ironic since these same professionals prided themselves on their basic purpose—which was communication.

In addition to her indecision over her academic life, she was troubled, yet simultaneously relieved, as she thought of how she had changed since she left Arkansas. At that time, she now knew, she was so naive to think she'd just get into her little 1984 Pontiac Sunbird and be able to drive away for a totally new life. In her mind, she imagined she might even go for some auditions in Hollywood while she was a graduate student. After all, she had acted in several productions at the University of Arkansas, the Sager Creek Arts Center, the Rogers Little Theater, and the Springdale Little Theater group. Everyone complimented her work and said she could be a big-time movie star if she wanted to. As usual though, Mama had talked her into THE PLAN. When she had her last big crisis, now considered tiny compared to her current one, she was eighteen.

She remembered lying in her waterbed in her bedroom in Tontitown and crying. When her Mama heard her, as usual she had to come in and ask what was going on. She wished Mama would give her a little space. Kimberly knew Mama loved her very much, but she expected perfection from both her and

Chris. Any little deviation from either her or her brother sent Mama into a tailspin of concern about what SHE had done wrong. The trouble was, their conversations always got back to Mama and what she was experiencing, not her. She longed for true friends who would listen to her and give her advice.

"Tell me what's wrong, Kimberly. Are you sick?" Mama questioned.

"No, nothing's wrong. Just leave me alone for a while."

"Don't tell me nothing's wrong. What is it, baby?" Mama went into her little girl voice.

"It's just that I want to go to California to live!"

After getting over the immediate shock, since this was the first her Mama had heard of this idea, they talked it through and agreed that Kimberly should continue her degree at the University of Arkansas, go to summer school, and graduate at age twenty.

"That way," her mama reasoned, "you won't have to wait tables like all the aspiring actors out there. You might want to teach in high school or even go to graduate school. The hours are flexible, and you'd still be able to go on auditions."

Mama had won out, and Kimberly had followed the plan to the letter. In late August of 1989, she had gotten into the car, all packed with the TV/VCR combination, linens, dishes, cookware, etc. and headed west with her best high school friend, Lorie, who wanted to drive out with her and then fly back to Arkansas. By that time, she had been accepted as a graduate student at USC. Mama and Dad had gone out to L.A. a few months earlier and rented a room for her in South Central L.A., just blocks from the campus. She was ready.

Reality soon set in, however, with the busyness of her schedule. As a graduate student, her reading and her assistant- ship took hours and hours each day. She was pleased at first with her independence and made friends with the others who were renting rooms in the house. After her boyfriend, Brian, was left back in Arkansas, Tony from England was her next serious attraction. They had soon slept together, but it seemed immediately that she was disturbed by his protectiveness and hovering like a mother hen over her. He was always knocking on her door, several times a day.

On one occasion, as he was leaving, he asked her, "Why don't you ever come to my room and knock on the door?"

"How can I?" she responded, "when you're always com- ing here and knocking on my door?"

She was also disturbed by his declaration that he was an atheist. While she realized she hadn't been that close to God either since she got to California, now that Sunday school and church weren't mandated by Mama, she still was a believer. After a few months, they broke up, but it was hard to hear Tony down in his room now with another woman. The walls were so thin in the house; nothing could be kept a secret from the others.

At least she had a new best friend in California, Patti, from Chicago. Since she also lived in the house, they spent hours gig- gling and talking about their master's work at USC and about the others in the house. Patti had a married boyfriend and was frequently asking Kimberly's advice about whether to maintain the relationship or break up.

Kimberly soon met Osbed, an Armenian, who was also a grad student at USC. She had another brief relationship with a guy named David, but that had gone down the tubes quickly. In many ways, Osbed was a tender lover who seemed to be getting quite serious about making their relationship permanent. She knew it was so when he took her home with him one Thanksgiving and she met his family. Soon after, he proposed.

She thought seriously about his offer of marriage, but she truly wasn't experiencing anything sexually in the relationship. She began to wonder if there was something wrong with her. About this time, in her academic classes she was becoming familiar with the writings of the feminists and the possibilities for a same sex relationship. For the first time in her life, she wondered if she were a lesbian.

As a Christian, she struggled with the biblical admonitions against such a life. Hell, damnation, and all that—she thought.

But at the same time, she became increasingly convinced that she was indeed attracted to women, not men. She had a curious experience back in Arkansas one day as she was in a lingerie shop getting fitted for a black, sexy garment she needed for a play she was in. The saleswoman had been fussing and feeling the garter belt while it was on, and Kimberly thought, "Oh, she must be gay."

She was so naive at that time that she never even considered the possibility that she herself was the gay one. Her mama and she had never talked about the subject, and Mama was always asking, "Do you think any of the boys in your classes are cute?" She had grown up believing there was no other possibility for love other than heterosexual love.

Soon she had met someone in L.A. It was just before the Thanksgiving holiday in 1991, and she was flying back to Arkansas to tell her parents she was gay. She dreaded coming out because she knew how conservative her parents were. She felt she couldn't be free, though, until she told them.

She thought she would tell her secret to her Mama first and waited for a good time to do so in the brief four days she had at home. As usual, her Dad had to work the Friday after Thanksgiving, and Kimberly and Mama had gone for a day trip to Eureka Springs, a small resort town just an hour away. On the way back, it was raining heavily when Kimberly ventured out into the life path that could go one way only.

"Mama, I don't want you to get upset," she said, "I want you to think about this for a while—I've started dating a woman in California."

The reaction from her Mama was immediate and cruel. She burst into tears and started weaving back and forth on the narrow, winding two-lane highway. As Kimberly thought about the huge scene later, she realized that she had actually chosen the worst possible time—when they were both tired from a long day. She smiled wryly, though, as she thought about the macro-cosm of the scene—the thunder and lightning were certainly appropriate to the emotional explosions inside the car.

When they got home, her Mama told her they would talk more the next morning. For the first time in her life, her Mama had not told her she loved her as they went to bed in their separate bedrooms. They were all emotionally devastated by the evening. The next day her Mama gave her a letter that said basically that she was just being rebellious, and certainly sinful, in her choice.

It was now spring, and the storm in the family had been relatively calm since Thanksgiving, but she knew her parents were still struggling over the idea of her being a lesbian. She had been surprised, however, to hear her mother say that she herself had known it all along, but she had prayed to God that it wouldn't be true. As she thought about her childhood, Kimberly had just thought a lot of girls were tomboyish like herself, always wishing they were boys instead of girls. It had never occurred to her that sexuality was involved in any way. But then she had been in a Christian school since third grade, and issues of sexuality were simply not discussed either in or outside of the classroom.

Her parents had surprised her with a graduation present for her master's degree and for passing her comps—a new red Toyota. They were still hoping that this whole identity issue was just a passing fancy and that it would go away in time. She knew it wouldn't, so basically, they were still at an impasse. She knew in her mind that she couldn't complete her doctoral degree: she hated everything about the idea of teaching forever in a stuffy university setting and developing the elitist attitude she witnessed every day with her professors and fellow students. It also seemed inexorably connected to her sexuality. She would have to be herself, or she couldn't go on at all in this life.

At this point in her memories of the past few years, her cat, Grimalkin, meowed at the bathroom door. Kimberly looked above the steam in the bathtub, saw the razor blade that she had been using, ironically she now thought, for looking feminine. She thought briefly about killing herself: it would be relatively easy this way. She could take up the razor, slit her wrists—which would bleed easily in the hot water—and leave the emotional pain she was experiencing.

She realized immediately, however, that she needed help. She slipped out of the bathtub and went to the phone. It was a Saturday morning, and she knew Mama would be home.

"Mama," her voice began to crack, and there was a long silence before she could continue. "Mama," she tried again, "I'm... I'm... not feeling... (she groped for the right word) ... very well. I want to come home."

"Kimberly, your dad and I will be right out there to get you," her Mama said simply without bothering to seek answers at that moment to the myriad of questions she must have had in her mind. She simply heard the desperation in her daughter's voice.

Chapter Seventeen
"You'll Still Be the Sweetest Little Baby in Town."
—Kimberly Michelle Brandom (1999)

Kimberly sat on her futon while her Mama sat across the room in her favorite chair while at her place, the dark green recliner. It was a Sunday morning, and Mama had just returned from visiting Bethany Presbyterian Church in her neighborhood there in Queen Anne. It would be Mama's last visit to the church in a while since she and her Dad were heading north to Alaska after a week's visit down south with her brother, Chris. Kimberly was aware that Lisa wanted to talk to her about where she was now at this time of her life spiritually. She really didn't dread the conversation, although at this point she had come to believe that one's beliefs were personal and private. They didn't necessarily have to be shouted from the rooftop, and one didn't have to be praying publicly all the time like her teachers and fellow students at Shiloh believed when she was growing up.

"I know that you've had struggles and had some spiritual

battles, so tell me a little bit about that. Have you changed in any of your original beliefs?" Mama inquired to get the conversation going.

"I no longer believe the Bible is the Word of God only, but Word of God filtered through men, so that's how you and I differ. . . just because of the Bible's being anti-sexist, anti-gay, anti-anything. The Truth is that God is love, for the most part, and the Bible, a lot of Paul's writing especially, is very negative. I associate that with Paul himself. I discovered that fact when I was with Stephanie, and we went to the Metropolitan Church (which we didn't like very much), and the pastor started the sermon in a way which I would think of as a traditional Baptist sermon. She said, 'Well, I prayed last night that God would speak through me.' I couldn't concentrate on the rest of her sermon because I got to thinking that what she said really made sense— that she would pray that—but how many others of different denominations, different backgrounds, and different languages throughout the country were saying the exact same thing. That's when I came to my theory (not really mine since a lot of people believe this way) that the Bible is filtered through men. Her sermon was important, and God also speaks through the Baptist preachers, but when it goes through humans it changes; it becomes part of them and part of God."

Mama replied,"Ummm. . . I know my friend Dollie always struggles with those same issues as well. She doesn't know how much is God and how much is the culture and history of the day."

"When I was an undergraduate student and just getting away from Shiloh, I started thinking about Christianity and tried to think about it from an outsider's position. I think it *could* be seen as a big scam...what bigger scam than to say only by faith can you come to God! Still that leap of faith is an interesting one...yesterday on NPR I heard a story about a lot of scams in the Christianity community. Did you hear that, Mom?"

"No, I haven't."

"Basically, it was saying people prey on others in the church with get-rich-quick schemes and the fact that people are more gullible because they take that leap of faith initially, and then they believe that of everyone else in the same pew at church. They're very inclined to believe in those con artists because they attend the same church. Then a year or so later they skip town."

"That does have to do with trust. Remember our neighbor down the street in Tontitown."

"The one who had the Amway pyramid scam?"

"Yes, that one."

"Back to the topic at hand though, there's that central belief that it's difficult for most people to have faith. For me, I believe, I was born with it almost—that ability to have faith. Back when I was in graduate school, I tried to be an atheist, or stop believing in God, but it was completely impossible because everything I know was founded on a belief in God."

Mama added, "One idea I've been thinking about a lot

lately, based on some readings we do in American Literature and others, is that there is one God but maybe He has provided different cultures with different ways to know Him."

"That's what Sheri and I discuss also. I believe my way is through Jesus Christ; for others it may be through Budda or other sources."

"But we can never know. We can have glimpses, insights, or illuminations, but as humans we can never know the full Truth."

"I know if I were God I wouldn't have earthquakes, but on the other hand, it's difficult to come to God. If life were easy, it would be incredibly easy to believe in God, but when your loved ones die, or are hurt or unhappy . . . ," Kimberly stopped talking for a moment since she wanted to meditate on what she had just said, but Mama began to press for more.

"Kimberly, are there any other thoughts you have about spirituality right now?"

"Oh, there's a bumper sticker here in Seattle that's popular: Jesus Christ, save me from your followers. That's actually very good because sometimes the followers are the most vicious (although that's no excuse not to come to God), but many times Christians keep people from coming to God. We were watching on TV the black music awards, and there was a Christian African-American guy receiving an award. He told about an experience on the plane when he was in first class. He and another man were chatting and being friendly when the guy asked him, 'What do you do?' He replied, 'I'm a gospel singer,' and instantly all communication was cut off. He was saying we as Christians need to make our reputations so good that people *want* to talk to us.

"Anything else you want to share?"

"Again, I don't see anything that Jesus taught that was negative—just Paul. *The Color Purple* was important to me in graduate school—when Alice Walker tells of seeing God in a field of purple flowers."

"What about if you had a child—would you want to send that child to a public school which wasn't very good or a private Christian school?"

"Sheri and I have talked about that. We'd probably opt for a Christian school but not a conservative one. We think a liberal one like Episcopalian. We think we would like to give the child, whether it be a boy or a girl, education about religions or denominations but let him or her decide at a later date."

"There's some research out there which suggests that it's best to tell a child directly to say no to such things as drugs and alcohol—in other words, to have a more proactive role in their decision making."

"We would definitely want to tell the child what we believe. I would certainly want to raise a child with a belief in God."

"My last question is about you again. When you were dealing with coming out, did you ever feel that God had rejected you personally?"

"No, I never thought He didn't love me. I had already dealt with those spiritual questions earlier in graduate school, so coming out was another issue altogether. For me it was almost a spiritual experience, the incredible freedom that I felt not having to hide this from myself and others. I knew He loved me, but I couldn't live without parental love too."

"It just took us a while to reconcile everything. But now we have."

"Now we have."

One must remember the past—and the shadows within it. Then at the appropriate time, she must rise up and take the hand of the one who has gone before her and the tiny, chubby hand of the one who will follow in her footsteps. She will sing this time, "Speak, little baby, do say a word; Mama's gonna buy you the whole wide world. If that whole wide world is yours, Mama's gonna buy you . . . ."